The believer's inner life dictates his outer life. A Christian veneer will not suffice in the tough battles facing us today; we need to fill our minds with the Word of God and our hearts with the power and love of His Holy Spirit.

Sherwood Wirt's marvelous book provides an inspiring guide in cultivating that inner life. This new volume I highly recommend for Christians who are serious about living out their faith.

—Charles W. Colson

THE INNER LIFE OF THE BELIEVER

Sherwood Eliot Wirt

First Printing, January 1989

Published by
HERE'S LIFE PUBLISHERS, INC.
P. O. Box 1576
San Bernardino, CA 92402

Library of Congress Cataloging-in-Publication Data
Wirt, Sherwood Eliot.
    The inner life of the believer : building the fortress of your
heart / Sherwood E. Wirt
    p.   cm.
    Includes index.
    ISBN 0-89840-242-5
    1. Spiritual life.   I. Title.
BV4501.2.W573   1988
248.4—dc19   88-30156
CIP

Unless otherwise indicated, Scripture quotations are from the *King James Version.*

Scripture quotations designated NIV are from *The Holy Bible, New International Version,* © 1978 by the New York International Bible Society, published by the Zondervan Corporation, Grand Rapids, Michigan.

For More Information, Write:
L.I.F.E.—P.O. Box A399, Sydney South 2000, Australia
Campus Crusade for Christ of Canada—Box 300, Vancouver, B.C., V6C 2X3, Canada
Campus Crusade for Christ—Pearl Assurance House, 4 Temple Row, Birmingham, B2 5HG, England
Lay Institute for Evangelism—P.O. Box 8786, Auckland 3, New Zealand
Campus Crusade for Christ—P.O. Box 240, Colombo Court Post Office, Singapore 9117
Great Commission Movement of Nigeria—P.O. Box 500, Jos, Plateau State Nigeria, West Africa
Campus Crusade for Christ International—Arrowhead Springs, San Bernardino, CA 92414, U.S.A.

To Michael and Sandra MacIntosh

Acknowledgments

Together with my personal walk, a lifetime of drawing upon the thoughts of others has been tapped for this internal examination of the Christian life. Acknowledgments therefore present a monumental problem. It would be only proper, however, to mention with thanks the help provided in the preparation of these pages by a number of fellow-writers; by my wife, Ruth; and by the editors of Here's Life Publishers. As to Dr. Billy Graham's foreword—what can I say? I refer the reader to the title of the fourteenth chapter, which says it best. And I would express gratitude for the kind comment of my friend, Mr. Charles Colson.

Those who have read my earlier published efforts may find a thought which has been expressed before. The bulk of this material, let me assure you, has never previously appeared in print. Its substance is what I have been articulating publicly and privately wherever the Lord, in His wisdom, has chosen to deploy me over the past seventeen years.

S.E.W.
Poway, California
January, 1989

Contents

Foreword 9

1. Your Private Castle 11

2. The Love of the Spirit 19

3. The Fourth Tree 29

4. Down v. Up 37

5. Up v. Down 45

6. The First Love 53

7. The Great Distraction 61

8. The Other Kind of Prayer 71

9. When God Says 'Wait' 83

10. What is the Inner Life for? 93

11. Battle Flags 101

12. Soul Food 109

13. In v. Out 119

14. A Touch of Class 127

Notes 135

Index 139

Foreword

Far too often we have forgotten the truth that God not only wants to change our outward behavior but our inner lives. In fact, without inward transformation by the Holy Spirit there is no lasting outward hope.

Few writers have captured this truth so vividly and perceptively as my longtime friend and associate, Dr. Sherwood Wirt. In a series of highly readable but thoughtful chapters, he points out from the Bible what God wants to do in our inner lives, and explores the barriers which keep the Holy Spirit from breaking us out of our pride and selfishness and filling our lives with true love. It is a book which contains an essential and urgent message—a message which needs to be heard and heeded if Christians are to become the salt and light in the world that God intends them to be. I highly commend this book.

—Billy Graham

O·N·E

With this inner life, we are magnificently equipped to face whatever life throws at us.

YOUR PRIVATE CASTLE

A mighty fortress is our God.
—Martin Luther

The inner life of a believer is a pearl of great price. To start living it requires that we liquidate everything we own and place it on the line. Whatever else we value can go, but this must remain, or there is no life worth living for a Christian. But once we have it, once it is really ours, we have that which the world can neither give nor take away, and the devil himself is powerless to molest it.

This inner life is like a castle built upon a rock, protected on all sides by sheer walls. It is a bastion, an unassailable fortress; nothing can disturb it. Sin, evil, wrongdoing of all kinds are kept outside. Missiles, rockets, thermonuclear explosions, environmental poisonings cannot penetrate the atmospheric shield that surrounds the castle. Hijackings, kidnapings, drugs, murders, wars, bombings, treacheries, espionage, racism, immorality, child abuse, wickedness and violence of whatever form can find no entrance; nor can jealousies, naggings, quarrelings, arguings, or unkind whisperings.,

Obviously this castle is different from the medieval castles we read about in story books. Those castles, with their flanking towers, ramparts, palisades and battlements, were hardly equipped to withstand the assaults of today's long-range missiles with their nuclear warheads. In fact, they couldn't even hold out against the battering rams and siege artillery of their own day.

The castle we have in mind is not like the Tower of London, or the famous castles of the Rhine, or Stirling, or Caernarvon. For one thing, it has no dungeon. Nor is it a fairy castle conceived by the imagination out of thin air. In the middle ages the castle was the fortress and home of a lord who built it to protect his lands and defend his family and followers from attack. The castle we have in mind is a citadel to ward off the catapults and flaming brands of the evil one, but it is more than that. Within its walls we seek to nurture and protect the spiritual communication that gives meaning and vitality to everything we set out to do in our day-to-day existence. We learn the innermost secret of the universe, the purpose for which we were created. For our castle is a castle of love, and the Lord of the castle is God Himself.

Without this inner life our Christianity is just another hoop to jump through in the circus of existence. Religious duties are a bore; the Bible seems a wasteland. Frustrations and disappointments that plague other people, plague believers also. We find we cannot cope. The assurances we get on Sunday are dissolved into gruel by Monday noon, leaving us hungry. Life is reduced to a macabre existence.

With it, we are magnificently equipped to face

whatever life throws at us. At the center of our being, where we most authentically live, we remain equable and serene. Let the planet explode, let the constellations slip their orbits, let the universe itself stand on its ear; it doesn't matter. Our lives are hid with Christ in God.

To the world our castle does not exist except as a figment of the religious imagination. It is rejected as an image created by hyperactive minds, an island of escape, a retreat from life, a phantasm decorating the pious landscape. Thus it helps the world to "account for" (but does not explain) the strange, narrow views that Christians hold about ethics and morals, life and death, time and eternity.

For the believer the inner life is reality. It gives meaning and significance to the cosmos. Its chief characteristic is that it is impenetrable and therefore invulnerable; nothing can disturb it. To illustrate, take the dearest thing on earth to any believer. It may be a person or more than one person. It may be one's life work. It may be one's greatest accomplishment, the fruit of years of struggle. It may be a good name, a reputation earned in the community or the nation. Suddenly in a fraction of time it is wiped out. A rich and happy life is marred or even destroyed, and the victim is left grieving and desolate.

Or perhaps one's physical suffering has increased to the point where the victim cries out to God to be released. The ravages of pain and illness are such that life is no longer bearable, and the prospect of death seems a blessing. Even against these forces, the believer finds that his castle is impregnable. He cries out with Job, "Though he slay me, yet will I trust him."[1] And he sings the words of Martin Luther:

> "Let goods and kindred go,
> This mortal life also,
> The body they may kill,
> God's truth abideth still;

Chapter One

His Kingdom is forever."

What do the "big bangs" of outer space matter? The inner life remains untouched. The believer's fellowship is with the Lord of the castle, and stands inviolate.

The castle is not a prison. It has walls and a moat for protection, but it has also a drawbridge and a single entrance. That is the gate of love. Everything else is denied access; even Satan is reduced to prowling around outside the moat; yet the believer himself is free to go in and out. His movements are unrestricted because wherever he goes, *the castle goes with him.* He is not always dwelling within its walls, but it is always there, and at any time he can return by just offering a prayer. He crosses the moat, hoists

---

We will find that the Christian life is an exciting adventure, never dull.

---

the drawbridge, lowers the portcullis and closes the iron-studded double doors. Then, secure against outside interference, he resumes his conversation with his Lord.

Life within the castle itself consists of a pure and beautiful relationship with the Master of the Keep. The believer and his Lord are inseparable. There are times of speaking and listening, study times, meal times, exercise times, even play times. We shall look into these activities as we explore the different parts of our castle: the turrets, the Great Hall, the keep, the watchtower, the armory, the chapel, the loopholes, and the rest. We will find that the Christian life is an exciting adventure, never dull; that God's mercies are always new and fresh for those who love Him.[2] The underhanded remarks and innuendoes of the world are missing; it is a castle without dungeons. And no matter how fierce the storms without, and how confusing the turmoil in the vortex of the human power struggle, inside the walls of our castle we shall always find warmth and cheer amid calm and peace.

When the believer is engaged in activity outside the castle, and the opportunity arises, he tells others about the sanctuary he has found. He does not invite people through the gate, for in a real sense it is not his castle. Rather it is his mission to point others to their own castles, where the Lord is also in residence. Whenever he finds another Christian who is also living the inner life, a beautiful fellowship is established. But when, as often happens, he encounters Christians who are groping for some sort of stability in the midst of moral confusion and difficult circumstances, he talks to them about the filling of the Holy Spirit, which is the secret of the inner life and the key that unlocks the castle gate.

Perhaps he tells them the story of John Tauler, the fourteenth-century Dominican monk whose writings so greatly influenced Martin Luther. One day, we are told,[3] Tauler was walking in the city of Strasbourg when he met a peasant. By way of greeting the man, the monk said, "God give you a good day, my friend."

"I thank God I never have a bad day," answered the peasant.

Astonished, Tauler was silent a moment, then tried again. "God give you a happy life, my friend."

The peasant replied, "I thank God I am never unhappy."

"Never unhappy?" cried Tauler, bewildered. "What do you mean?"

"Well," came the response, "when it is fine I thank God, when it rains I thank God, when I have plenty I thank God, when I am hungry I thank God, and since God's will is my will, and whatever pleases Him pleases me, why should I say I am unhappy when I am not?"

Tauler looked at him with awe. "Who are you?" he asked.

"I am a king," said the peasant.

"A king? Where is your kingdom?"

The peasant smiled. "In my heart," he whispered.

This book was written at the request of a Christian publisher who has a pastoral concern for his readers. I undertook it with the same purpose in mind. The intent is not to entertain or impress you, but to help you in your inner life. As far as God is concerned, if something doesn't take place there, it doesn't take place at all, no matter how much religious running around we do.

Beyond the historical and didactic and prophetic aspects of the Bible there are vistas of rich communion with the living God, vistas of time and eternity that can lift us out of ourselves, and envelop us in a joyful radiance that gives a glow to all of life around us.

A genuine miracle of the twentieth century is that many individual believers and churches are discovering that joy is one of the marks of a Spirit-filled life. Just as the Galilean disciples found a new kind of happiness in being with Jesus (why else did they respond to the command, "Follow me"?) and the early young followers of Francis of Assisi found that same exhilaration, so many Christians today are peeling back the layers of religious tradition and finding that the gospel is what it claims to be: glad tidings of great joy.

Jesus had a poor opinion of people who were solemn for the sake of solemnity. "Be of good cheer," He said, and the apostle Paul added, "The Lord loves a hilarious giver." Jesus singled out for rebuke those who wore "long faces" and sought to impress others with their piety. What He did in going to the cross, He did "for the joy that was set before

Him." Jesus was supremely a good person to be around, and many churches today have given up their funereal atmosphere and are becoming good places to be around. That is the work of the Holy Spirit.

But who is the Holy Spirit? What does He do? More importantly, what does He do for us? The answer lies in the Bible, but like a lot of other people who read the Bible, I missed it. You will remember Jesus' two stories of costly treasure.[4] One man found the treasure accidentally in a field, and sold all he had to buy the field. The other man, a merchant, was looking for pearls, and found one so expensive that he sold everything he owned to buy it.

It may be that you did not realize what you had been missing in the Christian life, when you accidentally came across this book. It may be that you thought you had it all, wrapped in a kind of comfortable orthodoxy. But it was perhaps not a kingdom of the heart so much as a fairy kingdom, and it never really connected with life at the checkout counter.

You don't have to be a searcher or a scholar to find help in these pages. The ideas are not mine. They are not original. And you don't have to be a visionary. You don't have to be religious. You need not remember the name of the book, or the author, or the publisher. All that's required is that you be willing to sell off the old that didn't work, and reach out for something new that will.

PRAYER

Give me, Lord Jesus, a strong and vivid sense of your presence in this castle. Make it my true home. Let it be a fortress so impenetrable that all my useless, perverse and evil thoughts are left outside to wither and die, hammering futilely against the iron-studded double doors. Amen.

T · W · O

Such inner life as I had was filled with ambiguity . . . I loved the Lord, but had a love-hate relationship with some people.

THE LOVE OF THE SPIRIT

I cashed the check of Romans 5:5.
— Corrie ten Boom

Life, as the great European theologian Christoph Blumhardt once said, has no meaning in itself; it has meaning only in relation to God.[1] The word of the teacher in Ecclesiastes, "Meaningless! Meaningless! Everything is meaningless!" is a deadly accurate description of the universe when its Creator is removed from it.[2] In the same way the inner life of the believer does not depend upon himself; it flourishes only under the reigning lordship of the Holy Spirit.

In the last chapter we looked at the inner life as lived in a special kind of dwelling place which we called a castle. Very few castles are lived in today. If they are not designated as antiquated ruins, they must be drafty, uninviting places, impossible to heat, uncomfortable in warm weather, inhabited by bats, and plagued by bad plumbing and ancient wiring. But the castle we are describing is designed for a special purpose, and is not dependent upon chambermaids, scullions or repairmen. In our analogy we shall use only those aspects of the castle that suit our purpose.

At the heart of the social life in a castle is the Great Hall, where the lord of the manor sits. Here he entertains his guests, listens to the grievances of his subjects, issues commands, and sees to the proper ordering of the day. Here is the banqueting table, where he graciously presides over a sumptuous spread to which he has invited his friends.

Entertainment is provided by minstrels and storytellers, who were great favorites in medieval castles. And now I would like you to join me in my Lord's castle, and find a comfortable seat by the fire in the "solar" or "withdrawing room" behind the Great Hall, while I tell you a story.

In 1974, during my tenure as editor of *Decision* magazine, I attended the International Congress on World Evangelization in Lausanne, Switzerland. Together with several thousand other Christians from all over the world, I listened to the late Corrie ten Boom as she spoke of the working of God in her life. Miss ten Boom had been arrested by the Nazis during World War II for harboring Jews in her home in Holland, and was eventually transported with her sister Betsie to the notorious concentration camp for women in Ravensbruck, Germany. There Betsie died under the mistreatment she received. Through a clerical error, Corrie was released from the camp just before her age group was marked for execution. In fulfillment of a promise she made in the camp, she devoted the rest of her life to traveling around the world, telling people about Jesus.

Something Corrie said that day in Lausanne radically shifted the direction of my thinking about the Holy

Spirit. In Dr. J. D. Douglas's compilation of the Lausanne messages I have found the exact words Corrie used in her testimony, which follow:

> "I love the Germans. There is not a country where I work with such a great joy. My greatest friends live in that country, but sometimes I find people who have been cruel to me in the concentration camp. Once I saw a lady in the meeting and suddenly I thought, *That woman was the* [Gestapo] *nurse who was so cruel to my dying sister.* And there came hatred and bitterness in my heart. But when I felt that hatred and bitterness . . . I knew I had not forgiven her. And I know and you know that Jesus has said, 'If you do not forgive those who have sinned against you, my heavenly Father will not forgive you your sins.'
>
> "But I said, 'Oh Lord, I cannot, I am not able.' And suddenly I saw it. I cashed the check of Romans 5:5. I said, 'Thank You, Lord Jesus, that You have brought into my heart God's love through the Holy Spirit who is given to me and thank You, Father, that Your love in me is stronger than my bitterness and hatred.' I could go to that nurse and I could shake hands with her, and I had the joy to be used by the Lord to bring her to a decision for the Lord Jesus. What a joy!"[3]

Sitting there in Switzerland and listening to that story being told to a Christian audience, I wondered, *What is Romans 5:5?* Opening my little Greek-English New Testament I read, "The love of God is poured out into our hearts by the Holy Spirit which is given to us." The words jumped off the page. I thought, *Give me that again!* Of course I had read the passage many times before, but now it came alive, and in its freshness I discovered what I had unconsciously been searching for: a description of the work

21

of the Holy Spirit simply as love. I felt like standing on my chair and announcing my discovery to the entire International Congress on World Evangelization!

It was in December, 1971, two-and-a-half years earlier, that I was first exposed to the love of the Holy Spirit during the revival in western Canada. Several books have been written about the spiritual awakening that broke out first in Saskatoon, Saskatchewan, in October of that year, and later spread to churches in several provinces.[4] I encountered it one memorable night in Winnipeg, Manitoba.

During that brief episode I was reminded that God is love, and that the Holy Spirit is God. What the Canadians did for me was to complete the syllogism: They taught me that the Holy Spirit is love. To be filled with the Spirit, they said, is to be filled with love.

Now, I had listened to scholars and savants, and had read a few books on the subject, but for me this was plowing new ground. I had never thought of the Holy Spirit that way. I thought of Him as fire, as power, as wisdom, as unction, as truth, as grace, as one who brings reproof and conviction, as a mighty rushing wind, as the third Person of the Trinity—

But not as love.

It is one thing to hear preaching from the pulpit, and quite another to accept the message into one's heart as gospel truth. I had hesitated over this new teaching because it did not seem clear to me from Scripture. But Corrie ten Boom opened the Word to me in a way that established the point; and that summer day in Lausanne I, with her, cashed the check of Romans 5:5. In the days that followed I realized that the Spirit of God is actually the fire of love, the power of love, the wisdom of love, the unction of love, the truth of love. He spills the marvelous love of God into our hearts until our cups overflow, and we love everybody.

I have found added confirmation of this teaching in Romans 15:30, where the apostle Paul writes, "I exhort you, brethren, by our Lord Jesus Christ, and *the love of the Spirit,* to strive together with me in prayers." The love of the Spirit! And in Colossians 1:7 Paul writes to the Christians of Colossae with great joy, because his friend Epaphras has told him of their "love in the Spirit." Similar hints and allusions can be found throughout the New Testament, most notably in 1 Corinthians 13.

From the testimonies coming out of the Canadian revival it was evident that what happened in many churches during 1971-72 was the fulfillment of this promise: The love of God was poured out by the Spirit which was given, and the people were, quite amazingly, filled with love.

Some of the memorable teaching to come out of that revival has remained with me:

"You can't change anybody, but God can change you."

"Revival is nothing but God's finger pointed right at you."

"The church has been sweeping things under the rug. God is pulling back the rug."

"If you wish to be filled with the Spirit, you will have to deal with your problem." (How did they know I had a problem?) "Then you must ask God to crucify you." (I thought I did that when I became a church member.) "Once you have reckoned yourself dead and nailed to the cross, you can ask God to fill you with His Spirit, and thank Him, because He is going to do just that."

In the years following that revival, I wrote and published a good bit on this topic. I found it difficult to convey in words the excitement, the freshness, the glow that some of us knew. In a strange way a number of ordinary believers living in the Twin Cities of Minneapolis and St.

Paul received a fresh touch from the Lord, and it managed to break into our daily lives and put a tang in our witness. Churches invited us to visit their services. The general reaction was curiosity—people wanted to know what was going on. What did we claim to have that they didn't have? The answer to that was: Nothing!

For the next few years pick-up teams of volunteers, drawn from different churches, began traveling through the states of the Upper Midwest, visiting churches by invitation. We were simply people who liked to pray and who had been blessed in the revival afterglows. In these churches we would find ourselves on our knees with people we did not know, interceding for them before God till midnight or later. What heartaches were described! What tears we saw! What tender pleadings were offered! What testimonies given! And—what joy at the end!

In my own case, my home life and ministry were both transformed. It was as if the Holy Spirit had cut me a new set of orders. As if I received the word: "From now on you will cease to direct your life. I have taken it over. No more telephone calls to 'arrange' things, no more jockeying for position, no more self-promotion. You are no longer in charge." And then I was given one additional, and rather disturbing, piece of information: "You are no better than anyone else."

Actually I was more than willing to turn over my future to the Holy Spirit, since I had made rather a Benjamin's mess of my past.[5] But to say that I was no better than anyone else on the curb, or in the bars or the jails—people without faith and without hope—seemed most unreasonable. The fact that many people seem to agree with the above statement is just one more testimony to its truth.

In the years since then, the Scripture has confirmed that truth to me. I am a crude pot, formed of mud grubbed out of the soil of planet Earth and shaped into something like a utensil. God in His grace (I prefer to think of His grace rather than His wisdom) has condescended to place in this leaky vessel the life-conveying message of the gospel. The New Testament likens the message to treasure, and treasure is often defined elsewhere in the Bible as gold, silver and precious jewels.

As a believer, I am privileged to share this treasure with others. Thus the mud pot becomes a vessel (make that utensil) of honor, even while remaining a mud pot. "We have this treasure in earthen vessels, that the excellency of the power may be of God and not of us."[6] My mud is no better than anyone else's mud. If I need something for my self-esteem, it is that I am entrusted to carry the treasure.

The New Testament teaches me that it is not spiritual growth I need, but spiritual shrinkage...

That is another way of saying that the Holy Spirit has poured out His love into me. He is the one responsible for any good accomplished. He is the Extraordinary working in the ordinary.

I still remain a bit shy in spiritual gifts. That is not a cause for pride. But when I hear someone claiming to be closer to God than I for some reason, I begin to feel uncomfortable. It seems the gospel has been run off on a siding. People inform me, "I have grown so much spiritually in recent months." Where did they ever get the idea that they were supposed to grow spiritually? Certainly not from the first beatitude of Matthew 5: "Blessed are the poor in spirit, for theirs is the kingdom of heaven." The New Testament teaches me that it is not spiritual growth I need, but spiritual shrinkage; that God is looking not for spiritual giants but for spiritual pygmies, for persons of no spirit, so

25

He can fill them with the love of His Spirit.

Lack of love was my particular problem. Such inner life as I had was filled with ambiguity. I loved the Lord, but had a love-hate relationship with some people. Like millions of other believers, I needed something, but what? Look at us. We come to church every week, bringing our perplexities, but not really expecting much to be done about them. In church? Forget it. We like to go to church, generally speaking; we know worship is good for us; we admit we ought to behave better; but whether we ever will be better—well, we doubt it.

Of course, if we are slapped up against it, that's different. Then we cry out to God to do something. We batter the gates of heaven. We make vows and promises. We say we will change our ways, and mean it. But do you know what God does? He doesn't pat us on the head and welcome us back. He points us to the cross.

That is more than we bargained for, because when we find ourselves on the cross, we don't have any spirituality left to talk about. In fact, we don't have anything! We are empty. What is a cross? It is nails and a gibbet.

But as we look around the scene at Golgotha, we see that there is also a man there. He, too, is on a cross. And in our total nothingness, we turn to Him and repeat what a thief said to Him in his misery so long ago: "Lord, remember me!"[7]

And He does remember us. That is the mercy of God. He says to us, "Today, this day, you will be with Me."

It didn't happen to me that day. In fact, nothing happened when I prayed. One of the Canadians, a lady who prayed with me, remarked, "You didn't feel anything tonight."

"You're right," I told her. "If anything, I feel humiliated."

"The feeling will come later," she said. "And how!"

That ends this part of my story. And now it seems the minstrels and singers have arrived. If it suits your pleasure, we shall join the others in the Great Hall.

PRAYER

Father God, Creator and Shaper of all things, You made every cell in my body. Now take me into Your examining room and listen to my heartbeat. What does Your divine stethoscope say? Am I ready to accept the Lordship of the Holy Spirit? Perhaps You had better go through this teaching once more with me. Thank You in Jesus' Name.

*Until we are nailed to the cross, let's not
boast about being filled with the Spirit, or
carry on about the "victorious Christian
life" and "spiritual growth."*

THE
FOURTH
TREE

He that had no cross deserves no crown.
—Francis Quarles

In today's world, as in centuries past, castles are steeped in romantic legend. They take us back in reverie to the olden days of King Arthur and the Knights of the Round Table, where one of the more interesting customs, according to legendry, was the conferring of knighthood upon a young warrior. Before receiving the honor (known as the accolade) the candidate would spend a night in prayer vigil, kneeling before the cross in a private chapel. Such chapels were part of many medieval castles, and the cross was placed on a simple table against the far wall.

The conferring of knighthood by the sovereign usually took place in a castle ceremony, with the candidate kneeling and receiving the touch of a sword on his shoulder. Afterward, as in the crusades, the knight would sometimes have a cross decorating the escutcheon of his shield instead of a coat of arms. In Edmund Spenser's poem, "The Faerie Queene," the hero was called the Red Cross Knight.

The cross means many things to many people. What does it really mean to you?

Does it mean the suffering and death of Jesus Christ at a point in time? And did He do it for you? Did He shed His blood not just to fulfill prophecy, or to satisfy divine justice, or to overcome the devil, or to redeem the human race or some part of it, but first of all to take away your own sin? Did He, out of His great love for you, die on your behalf and in your stead, to forgive you and fit you for heaven?

If that is what the cross means to you, Hallelujah!

Perhaps, when you think of the cross, you think of it as a symbol of holiness. It stands for the purity and truth of God. When demons come out of their holes and caves, and immorality covers the earth like a swarm of locusts, and false messiahs and occult teaching infest the body politic, and evil powers threaten the human race, the cross remains the one incorruptible sign of God's truth. If you believe that, your thinking is on solid ground.

Or is the cross something more personal? Does it signify the kind of burden you yourself have been asked to bear? Does it remind you of the shame and reproach of Golgotha with which you, as a Christian, are called to identify yourself? Suffering comes to everyone; does the cross bring you to share also the sufferings of the Lord Jesus Christ? If so, you are in the grand New Testament tradition.

All of these meanings are valid and true and scriptural. But let me tell you of a fourth meaning that is also to be found in the Bible. It is immediately concerned neither with the vicarious sacrifice of Christ, nor with bearing His reproach, nor with the cross as the sign and symbol of truth.

Let me try to explain. Think of that hill of Calvary with three crosses on it. Now add another one. That is your cross. Are we on scriptural ground? Listen to these passages:

"I am crucified with Christ; it is no longer I that live, but Christ that lives in me" (Galatians 2:20).

"It may not be for me to boast except in the cross of our Lord Jesus Christ, through whom the world has been crucified to me and I to the world" (Galatians 6:14).

"For you died, and your life has been hid with Christ in God" (Colossians 3:3).

"We have had the sentence of death in ourselves, that we should not have trust in ourselves, but in God who raises the dead" (2 Corinthians 1:9).

What does all this crucifixion talk mean? Not that the self is dead, but rather that we are dead to self. Please note that this has nothing to do with self-esteem! We'll get to that later. What we are dealing with here is a central core of gospel truth: It is not enough to survey the cross, to be near the cross, to kneel at the cross, or even to bear the cross. According to the Scriptures we need to be nailed to the cross.

Until we are, let's not boast about being filled with the Spirit, or carry on about the "victorious Christian life" and "spiritual growth." Don't be fooled. Spiritual growth as human achievement is not the gospel. Crucifixion is the gospel. It is the one and only starting point for Spirit-filled Christian living.

Well, how do we go about having the experience of crucifixion? What does it involve? Beating our breast? Announcing to the world that we are nothing but trash? That is missing the point completely. When we join Christ at Calvary it means we are all through being off-again, on-again Christians, picking up the cross one day, dropping it the next. Our nominal Christianity has a nail driven through it.

Crucifixion becomes for us neither a great victory nor a crushing defeat. It simply means we are no longer playing church, selecting whom we will like or dislike, using evangelical terminology to smokescreen our blatant self-interest. Nor are we presenting ourselves as upwardly-mobile models of perfection. What has crucifixion to do with perfection? All that is gone.

When we magnify our importance
out of all proportion, we harm His cause
by destroying our credibility.

Remember, the crucified ego is not really dead, it is only reckoned dead. Then how is it that our behavior is changed? The change is in the attitude we adopt toward ourselves. We stop taking ourselves seriously. That is a significant switch, because some religious people take themselves very seriously. They are at enormous pains to establish and protect their dignity, or (as they would put it) their credibility. Everything about them, their dress, their speech, their body language, is designed to impress others. They assume their vital importance to God and to everyone else, and adopt the words of Prince Hamlet:[1]

> The time is out of joint; O cursed spite,
> That ever I was born to set it right!

What a farce! As if everything depended on us! As if God who shaped the galaxies couldn't act independently of us, and in spite of us, if necessary. He has not rested all His hopes on us alone. When we magnify our importance out of all proportion, we harm His cause by destroying our credibility. Jesus told us to let the good works speak for themselves and bring glory to God. He also said, "Fear not, little flock, it is the Father's good pleasure to give you the kingdom."[2] We can climb down off our white horses. Paul's advice to the Roman Christians is apposite here: "Don't cherish exaggerated ideas of yourself or your importance, but try to have a sane estimate of your capabilities by the light of the faith that God has given you."[3]

The person who has allowed himself to be crucified with Christ, of course, feels nothing of this. He is beyond such feelings. In his own inner being he is unable, for the life of him, to take himself seriously. He knows himself too well. "I know," said Paul, "that nothing good lives in me, that is, in my sinful nature."[4]

Here then is the contrast: The unbeliever, or rather, the person who believes in himself, looks upon life as a congeries of confusion, a "tale told by an idiot,"[5] a haphazard, meaningless succession of events. And since life seems to make no sense, he often regards this vale of pain and darkness not as a tragedy but as a monstrous, bitter joke.

Thomas Hardy, the agnostic English novelist, expressed his view of life as a joke at the end of *Tess of the D'Urbervilles*, as he has the girl Tess lying dead. His closing word was, "The President of the Immortals . . . had ended his sport with Tess."

A popular song of depression days was even more specific:

> Life is just a bowl of cherries;
> Don't take it serious (*sic*)
> Life's too mysterious . .

Often such a person looks upon himself as the one serious entity in his environment. Everything about him personally matters enormously; everything else is dog-eat-dog, a write-off. He feels an ethical responsibility to be responsible for himself and his existence, and that of his family; beyond that he refuses to go. Such is the essence of twentieth century existentialism.

The believer, by contrast, sees life from a completely opposite perspective. He takes life seriously because he takes the Bible seriously. He has learned from the New Testament that human existence is built on a foundation of love: love for God and love for other people. This love is only a reflection of the unsearchable love that fashioned the whole creation and reached down to us mortals in Jesus Christ. As Lady Julian of Norwich, the English nun, wrote in the fourteenth century, "The universe was made for love." This is the real message of Easter, the miracle of the empty tomb, and Pentecost.

Thus life to the believer is not a joke. Life is a proving ground, a road test. It is a serious business, getting ready for heaven. If there is a joke, it is the believer himself. He knows himself to be the least deserving, the least worthy, the least qualified. He contends with the apostle that he, rather than Paul, is the chief of sinners. How can he take himself seriously when there are so many others, far better equipped in every way to serve the Lord? He doesn't even belong in their company. Put him on a white charger, and send him out to fight the dragon, and he would look like Don Quixote astride his nag Rozinante. He is a joke. He is out of it.

To sum up: The believer takes life seriously, as from God; the unbeliever can make neither head nor tail of it. On the other hand, the unbeliever takes himself very seriously; the believer doesn't think that much of himself.

So life makes sense, even if the believer himself doesn't; and he is not about to jam the machinery of the galaxies by pretending otherwise. Instead he goes to the cross and opts out of the competition. He retires to his private castle, not to sulk and pout like a child with bruised

34

feelings, but to renew his dialogue with his Lord, and to
gain fresh momentum for the next challenge. What this
does to the believer's self-esteem, we shall see.

PRAYER

Lord, how do I begin to take myself less seriously?
Give me a sense of humor about myself. I know You can
bring in Your Kingdom without my help. In fact, I'm
probably getting in the way and kicking up dust. Grant
me some on-the-job training in practical living and self-
effacement, the kind that Jesus talked about, for His
sake.

Humility is not a contemporary virtue...Yet
there is no characteristic of the crucified life
more essential than a humble spirit.

DOWN
V.
UP

Still stands Thine ancient sacrifice
an humble and a contrite heart.
—Rudyard Kipling

I am Patrick, a sinner, the most awkward of country bumpkins, the least of all the faithful, and the most contemptible among very many."[1] That gives us a good Irish beginning for a gnarly subject!

Before we consider how self-esteem can possibly coexist with the filling of the Spirit, we need to take on the unpopular subject of humility, which has absorbed some hard licks in our Age of Assertiveness. If the crucifixion of the self, which we have been discussing, does not issue in some kind of humble or modest behavior, it is hard to imagine what it does do.

Historically, humility has always played a key role

in the inner life of a Christian. Patrick of Ireland (c.389-c.461), whose memory is honored today far beyond the Irish coasts (he himself was probably born in Scotland), is one Christian hero-saint who seems to have had a healthy inner life. His "castle" was always with him. Only two authentic documents have come down to us that contain Patrick's actual words, and one of them was his written confession of faith, which began with the remarkable statement that appears above.

Quite an opener for the man in whose name huge cathedrals have been erected, and for whom giant parades are staged in great cities each year during the month of March! A "contemptible sinner?" The "least of all the faithful?" It may seem strange that Patrick, a bishop who was highly esteemed in his lifetime, should have used such language to describe himself; and yet he was only reflecting what his New Testament had taught him.

Listen to these words of Scripture:

"Blessed are the meek" (Matthew 5:5).

"Walk humbly with your God" (Micah 6:8).

"In lowliness of mind let each esteem others better than themselves" (Philippians 2:3).

"Put on humbleness of mind" (Colossians 3:12).

"Be clothed with humility" (1 Peter 5:5).

"God resists the proud, but gives grace to the humble" (James 5:16).

Thomas à Kempis (c.1380-1471) wrote, "A true understanding and humble estimate of oneself is the highest and most valuable of all lessons . . . We are all frail; consider none more frail than yourself."[2]

Francois Fénélon (1661-1715) wrote, "All the saints are convinced that sincere humility is the foundation of all virtues. That is because humility is the daughter of pure love."[3]

But humility is not a contemporary virtue. It is in low repute in the media and just about everywhere else. It appears out of touch with the twentieth century, and will probably be even more unpopular in the twenty-first. Yet there is no characteristic of the crucified life, as the New Testament describes it, more essential than a humble spirit. To be modest, meek, self-effacing, unpretentious, to shun the limelight (or better yet, to be unaware of it)— these qualities are considered direct fall-out from the life of renunciation known as self-crucifixion.

But humility, by its very nature, presents a problem to human beings. My friend the late George Edstrom illustrated it when he would ask solemnly, "Have you heard my sermon on humility?" With tongue in cheek he would add, "It's the greatest sermon I ever preached!"

Let's assume we find ourselves discussing with friends the question of "who gets the credit?" in a certain matter. For once we drop our swagger, adopt a humble stance and back off. No sooner do we do so than a fresh temptation stands in our way. We become very quietly but inordinately proud of what we have done. But being Christian, we realize what has happened—the devil has trapped us. So with great strength of character we shake him off and force ourselves to become ashamed of our pride. This results in a new humility which only feeds our ego afresh. We know now that we really are humble. There seems to be an infinite regression here, and no way out of it. Samuel Taylor Coleridge pointed out that "the devil's darling sin is pride that apes humility."[4]

Perhaps that is why the Lord never tells us in His Word that we are to pray for humility. Instead we are to humble ourselves (2 Chronicles 7:14), which is quite a different thing. We must find our own way to the cross. Before His execution, Jesus told His disciples that no one was

39

taking His life from Him; He was laying it down of His own choice. In the same way the crucifixion of the self is the result of a deliberate decision on our own part. We make up our mind to back out of God's way. In fact, we jump, lest we be run over. God doesn't want to hurt our pride, He wants to kill it. But He prefers to do it by letting us do it, which is for us far more prudent than asking God (or anyone else) to do it for us.

Fred Smith, who has a wonderful way of putting things, says, "Humility is not denying the power you have, but admitting that the power comes through you and not from you." Pride, on the other hand, assumes that the power is a natural attribute of the person in question, is inherent in said person, and should be credited entirely to the same. Pride is even willing to ascribe to such a person the properties of divinity. As Bertrand Russell wrote, "Every man would like to be God if it were possible; some few find it difficult to admit the impossibility."[5]

The Beatles announced in their heyday, "We're more popular than Jesus!" Today one of them is dead and another has sued the rest. Mohammed Ali taunted the world with his "I'm the greatest" routine. Who would exchange places with him today? Hercules, Tarzan, the Red Shadow, Superman, Batman, Rambo, the Bionic Woman—all these are the votaries of pride, the escape images of human craving for power over others. Ridiculous as these fictional characters may seem when examined closely, they are wimps when their pretensions are compared to the struttings and trumpetings of the religious community.

From the autocratic pagan priests of ancient Egypt to the haughty churchmen of today, scattered among the various branches of Christendom; to the haughty imams of Islam and the haughty monks of Buddhism, and all the other haughty religious types in our global cultures—the history of religion is in large part the history of human pride and arrogance. It is a story of individuals using the perennial human quest for the supernatural as a stepladder to boost their own efforts to achieve power and fame.

Religion may well be the easiest route for those persons to take who wish to lord it over their fellows. If so, that might explain why religious people so often are resistant to criticism. Christianity, it is said, is the only major religion to make a virtue of humility; but with rare exceptions, the higher up the ladder one manages to climb toward the empyrean glories, the less often one seems to find humility in evidence. "I beseech you," Oliver Cromwell once wrote to the General Assembly of the Church of Scotland, "in the bowels of Christ, think it possible you may be mistaken." But the churchmen assured him they were not mistaken.

---

*Giving the glory to God means
we simply pass the honors on to Him
and don't try to get a piece of the action.*

In our own time, John Stott has declared that "personal vanity lies at the root of most dissensions in every local church."[6] Personal vanity? Ah, yes . . . it is all too true. Dr. George Williams has called the history of the Christian church "the life of Peter writ large." Sometimes it seems it could also be called "the life of the sons of Zebedee writ large." It was James' and John's struggle to get to the top and stay there, that drew from Jesus His rebuke, "Whoever wants to become great among you must be your servant, and whoever wants to be first must be slave of all."[7]

God has a weapon that can change pride to humility in an instant of time. The apostle Peter named this weapon the "fiery trial."[8] It can bring about exposure, failure, humiliation, disgrace, the collapse of our carefully-built plans, the wiping out of our ambitious goals—everything, in fact, that we dread. Such an occurrence can prove to be a blessing; it may drive us straight into the castle to meet with our Lord. But here again, so often we fail to get the message. We think, in the darkness of our imaginations, that we are insured against any such calamity. If it does occur, we ignore the warning embedded in it. Instead we platoon our defense and begin to do a number on our detractors. We defend our "integrity" with all the vehemence of Job. We protest our innocence, we file a lawsuit, we waste the rest of our lives playing catch-up, seeking to reclaim and re-establish the ground we have lost.

To take the path of humility, the way of "dust and ashes" that Job finally found, is to go the way of the cross. Somewhere deep in our consciousness is a road that leads to the inner life. I have tried to describe it as a private road leading to a stronghold where images, profiles, reputations, and all the accoutrements of pride count for nothing; where we will find the Lord in residence, and that's all that matters.

By way of illustration: Have you ever noticed how difficult it is for Christians to accept praise or gifts? We're very poor at it. We resist; we protest; we feel much more comfortable giving than receiving. But true humility is unaffected by adulation, because it is unconscious of it. Humility has a clear understanding of how vapid are the honors of this world, and accepts them with appreciation but refuses to take them seriously. Giving the glory to God means we simply pass them on to Him and don't try to get a piece of the action. One of the aspects of Billy Graham's character that has appealed to me most has been the unsullied and unaffected way in which he has lightly received and borne the awards and honors heaped upon him. He unostentatiously lays them at Jesus' feet.

Before we pass from the subject of the cross, and our place on it, let us try to summarize what self-crucifixion means:

It means we have called at the heavenly brokerage, where we have turned in the worthless certificates of our self-conceit for the gold bullion of God's sufficiency.

We have exchanged our ungodly ambition for godly contentment.

We have traded our lifetime accumulations of ir- relevata for the pearl of the gospel treasure.

We have deflated our hot-air balloons, that we might be carried on the wind of the Spirit.

We have stripped off this world's nothings that we might be clothed in God's everything.

And we have thrown away the scorecard.

PRAYER

God of Orion and the Pleiades, who scatters the proud in the imagination of their hearts, hear the cry of your servant. I don't just want to be known as a humble person—I really want to be one. That being the case, please do what is necessary. I'd like a one-on-one inter- change with You at the cross; nothing else seems to work.

F·I·V·E

*It is possible to be a conceited, vainglorious
Christian, but such a person will
never find life easy.*

UP
V.
DOWN

*And he that strives to touch the stars,
oft stumbles at a straw.*
—*Edmund Spenser*

Many a feudal baron who proudly rode away to the wars boasting that his walled castle was unassailable, returned later to find it a smoking ruin. "Pride goeth before destruction."[1] But before we attempt to brand human pride as the origin, root and essence of sin, we should be fair and look at its good side.

Self-reliance, self-worth, self-esteem, self-respect. Yes, of course. Anything wrong with having a high opinion of one's own dignity? Anything wrong with the pioneer spirit? Why shouldn't we think enough of ourselves to try to do something about our situation? Can-do is what makes things happen. Are we mice or are we men? Are we wimps or are we women? Character is not built out of books or cardboard boxes; character is constructed from sound building materials in human flesh and blood. And character is what makes a proud civilization.

We know that in the normal course of life, we can't expect a person to tackle a job if he doesn't think he can do it. We also know that to scorn, to degrade, to demean, to humiliate, to break a person's spirit is a terrible punishment to inflict on anyone. On the other hand to encourage people to gird themselves, to roll up their sleeves, to accept a challenge, to bite the bullet, to find what's wrong and fix it, to have confidence in their ability to accomplish something, and even to glory in doing it—this is the quintessence of manhood and womanhood. This is pride in its good sense, which could be its true and proper connotation.

When the apostle Paul boasted (he apologized for using the term) of his hardships and sufferings on behalf of the gospel in his Second Letter to the Corinthians, he was not guilty of the sin of pride; rather he was glorying in what he had been privileged to endure for Christ, and was challenging the Corinthians to take their sufferings in the same spirit. "I will boast," he says, "of the things that show my weakness," and he quotes from the prophet Jeremiah, "Let him who boasts, boast in the Lord."[2] For us this is risky ground, for we are constantly tempted to insert our own egos into the God-talk. I remember hearing an old missionary describe one of his preaching visits to an oriental city. "God gave us a signal ministry there," he declared, and he set me to wondering: Is that word "signal" honoring to God or just more human self-flattery? It's a judgment call, as the sportscasters say. For the individual who has been to the Calvary of his own self-crucifixion, such a description of effort may well authenticate itself as Paul's did. We must not forget that Paul also did not hesitate to call himself the least of the apostles and the chief of sinners.[3]

46

Up v. Down

There is a kind of pride that brings out the best in people. I am proud to be a Christian, proud to be an American, proud to be a Californian, even proud to be asked to write this book. Yet I grew up with an excruciating sense of personal unworthiness. I was convinced that I didn't measure up to those around me, either physically or mentally, and it left me ashamed of myself. Then I struggled through the Depression of the 1930s, and knew what it was to beat the pavement of an unfriendly city and be told, "You're no good." I remember when men lived in sewer pipes, and were paid a pittance to dig holes and fill them up again. What blows to dignity, what contempt for the unemployed, what terrible feelings of being superfluous and unwanted! I was only one of the millions of victims of economic conditions in the 1930s, but I was desperately poor, lonely, unemployed and unhappy. To wake up every day aware that one's worth is inadequate to meet the demands of life, dreading the thought of pounding the pavement again, convinced that the world has no place for one to fit in—is to hit rock bottom.

But to emerge from all that years later with a sense of accomplishment, gratitude and relief is (if I may be permitted to say so) to know the good side of pride. Only, let's be clear: To speak in such a way is to avoid the whole subject of self-crucifixion. Pride, understood as "feeling good about what you've been able to do," has nothing to do with the inner life of the believer. We are talking about two different things—apples and oranges.

It may be true that the filling of the Holy Spirit helps a Christian to appreciate his own worth to God, and thus prepares him for a more useful role in life. But this is only the backwash of the Holy Spirit's work. The believer hardly notices it, and he certainly doesn't notice it when he is hanging on a cross.

When a man falls deeply in love with a woman, he

doesn't spend his time dawdling in front of a mirror and admiring himself. He has someone else to admire. When the Spirit of God pours out His love into the heart of a believer, that person is not about to become muscle-bound from patting himself on the back. Rather he has found other objects than self for his love.

God does not denigrate pride in its positive sense. The Bible has a hundred ways to illustrate the quiet feeling of competence that lies behind one's ability to do what he knows he has to do and can do. The apostle Paul's ministry was grounded on the assurance that Christ would help him finish what he had started. If that is what is meant by pride, we should certainly cultivate it and thank God for it.

But now turn over the coin.

To praise and exalt pride "of whatever extent" as the key to mental health; to claim that swaggering and boasting about oneself is only natural and therefore good; that "looking down your nose" at others will "enable you to do the extraordinary" (as is now asserted) is simply absurd. It is to mock at history, defer to the devil and deny the truth of God.

Pride in the dictionary sense of conceited and overbearing behavior is anything but the road to mental health. It brings out the worst in antisocial relationships. Such pride is not the answer to the human problem; it *is* the human problem. To say that Jesus Christ died for our self-esteem is to confuse the flesh with the Spirit. All of the major transgressions to inflict woe upon the human race—fear, greed, avarice, cruelty, lust, unbelief—can be traced to runaway pride. The warping of the heart that produced Tamerlane, Genghis Khan, Attila, Ivan the Terrible, Hitler and Stalin was brought about entirely by pride.

When the Pride Council of New York says that pride is "not a sin any more," it is really saying that "There is no

God any more"—at least, there is no longer the God of Abraham, Isaac and Jacob. Man (speaking generically) has assumed the driver's seat. But because he is a creature and not the Creator, man does not belong in the driver's seat. He is a usurper. Reinhold Niebuhr's words at this point are among the most brilliant he ever wrote: "Man is ignorant and involved in the limitations of a finite mind; but he pretends that he is not limited. All of his intellectual and cultural pursuits, therefore, become infected with the sin of pride. Man's pride and will-to-power disturb the harmony of creation."[4]

The apostle Paul's description of pride comes through most clearly in the King James version: "Professing themselves to be wise, they [the sinful mass of humanity] became fools, and changed the glory of the uncorruptible God into an image made like to corruptible man" (Romans 1:22-23).

---

*Nothing is easier to spot than
a selfish and egotistical personality.*

The sin of pride is far more complex than an athlete's normal pride in his team, or the average person's "feeling good about himself." It is unbelievable that the famous poem of Percy Shelley, "Ozymandias," should be cited to show that King Ozymandias was celebrating the "joys of prideful living," but that's what happened in a recent issue of *Harper's* magazine.[5] The truth is that Shelley's entire sonnet was an ironic commentary on the stupidity of human braggadocio and the emptiness of fame:

> I met a traveler from an antique land,
> Who said: Two vast and trunkless legs of stone
> Stand in the desert. Near them, on the sand,
> Half sunk, a shattered visage lies . . .
> And on the pedestal these words appear:

49

Chapter Five

"My name is Ozymandias, King of Kings:
Look on my works, ye mighty, and despair!"
Nothing beside remains. Round the decay
Of that colossal wreck, boundless and bare
The lone and level sands stretch far away.

Pride's warping, or to use a more familiar phrase, pride's curse, operates along quite natural lines. A man looks upon himself with esteem, and says to himself (to use the expression found on bumper stickers) "Damn, I'm good." This leads easily to an estimate which places him, in his own eyes, a notch higher than his fellows. Again, this quickly becomes what the ancient Greeks called *hubris,* that is, arrogance, insolence and excessive pride. *Hubris* in turn causes fear, for the proud person is always apprehensive lest something challenge his self-declared superiority. Fear, of course, invariably leads to avarice and greed, in the all-out effort to buttress one's position and make it secure. It also creates disdain, which leads to cruelty; and envy, which breeds aggression and war. A common concomitant of arrogance is lust, which is one part sexual desire and nine parts a desire to demonstrate one's pride by the domination of another.

Finally, pride results in unbelief, as the haughty individual finds it impossible to acknowledge anyone or anything greater than himself. The apostle Paul concludes, "Since they did not think it worthwhile to retain the knowledge of God, he gave them over to a depraved mind, to do what ought not to be done."[6]

And that is where we are today. Even some Christian psychologists are telling us that we should stop thinking of ourselves as sinners, but should assert our true worth and take pride in it. But the tragedy is that the more we emphasize the necessity of human pride, the more easily we forget that we are the creatures and not the Creator, and so the deeper we fall into deadly sin.

"According to the Bible," says Alan Richardson, pride consists in "rebelliousness which attributes to self the honor and glory that are due to God."[7] Unless this pride is recognized, identified, acknowledged, and taken to the cross of Calvary and nailed there, we will be as vulnerable as were Adam and Eve in the Garden of Eden when the serpent said to them, "You will be like God."[8]

Both in James and 1 Peter appear the words, "God resists the proud but gives grace to the humble."[9] It is possible to be a conceited, vainglorious Christian, but such a person will never find life easy. He will always be wading in molasses, for nothing is easier to spot than a snobbish and egotistical personality. What the Judgment will do with such a grandiose masterpiece of self-esteem is something else; praying Christians here on earth will be drawing on all the love they can get from celestial sources (1) to put up with the over-inflated individual, (2) to resist the temptation to avoid him, or (3) to discover a quiet Christian way to cut him down to size.

For the humble believer, Scripture tells us, things will go a lot easier. Regardless of his outward circumstances, in his mind and heart he will float down the river of life on an inner tube of divine grace right into the hereafter. Praise the Lord!

As to whether or not our pride is sin, the answer ultimately rests with each of us. The Christian knows the condition of his own heart. He measures it by the Word of God. Is he at peace? Is his conscience clear? Is he filled with the Spirit? Has he found his place of inner refuge, his castle where his Lord awaits him with a fire blazing in the hearth of the Great Hall? Then his personal life should reflect the modest, open, worshipful, loving stance of a humble creature of God who has been in the presence of his Creator.

Chapter Five

PRAYER

Great and Beloved Physician, my soul may need a biopsy. I ask that you do an exploratory on me and remove whatever is offensive to You. Look especially for traces of subtle pride; boasting is becoming a habit with me lately. I suspect that part of me may be malignant; if so, use the knife. I ask it in Jesus' name.

S·I·X

*Take your own survey of church members in
your acquaintance. Most will tell you that
they came [to church] because someone
loved them.*

THE
FIRST
LOVE

*Can I think that I love God with all my heart
while I hate that which belongs only to God...
which bears his image?*
— William Law

It ought to be apparent by now that our spiritual
pilgrimage is really a recapitulation of the gospel story.
We start out breathing the keen air of Galilee, looking to a
most exhilarating walk into the higher life, and we find ourselves slogging through the miasmic marshes of a rampant
selfhood in the accursed valley of Hinnom. Is crucifixion the
best the Christian life can offer? Are we to pass our days
hanging on the cross, or mourning with Mary in the garden
of Joseph of Arimathea?

Will there be for our inner spirit a personal resurrection, an ascension, a Pentecost? Can we look forward to a Christian life that is radiant and triumphant and truly glorious? And will this life be as available to the prisoner in a Gulag labor camp, or a hostage in a Shi'ite apartment, as to a comfortable citizen in a western country?

Perhaps we are as ready as we will ever be to look at a fresh interpretation of a passage of Scripture. If it should appear that our interpretation isn't all that fresh; that Origen or Gregory of Nazianzus suggested it centuries ago, our next printing will duly acknowledge the debt. The question remains: Is it true?

The inner life of the believer is at stake in this investigation. How is it lived? On what does it feed? What causes it to flourish? What makes it sicken? We have talked about a castle. Is it really possible, in what will soon be the twenty-first century, for us to live part of our lives shut up somewhere with our Lord? Isn't that putting a strain on our credulity? We have poked at the problem of self as a boy would poke at a rattlesnake, and we have seen some of the effects of both pride and humility. To pursue our research, look with me at the following verses in Revelation 2:1-4, and forgive me if I follow the Greek text in order to make some slight alterations in the more familiar translations. It might just be that the meaning will come through more clearly, and the inner life will take on substance, body and form.

> To the angel of the Ephesian assembly write: I know your efforts: your hard labor and your staying power. I know that you cannot bear evil ones, and that you have tested those who claim to be apostles, and are not, and have found them to be impostors. I know that you have suffered and endured, and that you labored without wearying for the sake of my name. But I have this against you, that you neglected your first love.

These words were spoken by Jesus Christ to his servant John on the island of Patmos, and were subsequently written by John to the Christians of Ephesus. Let's look at them carefully. Note the recognition given for hard work, for perseverance, for high moral standards and doctrinal purity. Lavish praise indeed, coming from the Head of the church! Note the particular reference to their efforts "for the sake of my Name," and the comment that they did not fall victims to battle fatigue. In each area of responsibility the Ephesians performed creditably. It was a handsome tribute to a worthy congregation.

But I have this against you, that you neglected your first love.

The climax came suddenly and unexpectedly. What in the world was Jesus talking about? Surely in the next sentence or two He would clarify His objection. But did He?

What about our love for each other?
We don't find many hymns in the hymnbook
about that.

He closed His brief letter with a warning to repent and a threat to "remove your lampstand out of its place." And for 2,000 years this enigmatic message has continued to tantalize the church, while a million teachers have attempted to explain what Jesus really meant by the "first love."

Let me be candid: I don't know what He meant. But neither it seems do such scholars as I have consulted. One Bible commentary states that "the first love was the love they had at the first." Can you believe it?

Many suggestions have been advanced over the centuries to unravel the expression. Such sermons as I have heard on the text nearly always describe the "first love" as the initial, rapturous encounter of the Christian with his Lord. Either they point to the believer's wondrous new sense of forgiveness associated with the surrender to the divine mercy, or else they talk about the close devotional walk, the intimate spiritual relationship of the disciple with his Master. The Ephesians had forsaken the precious fellowship, these sermons have pointed out. They no longer loved Jesus. Or to put it in more colloquial American terms, they had "got religion" but they "backslid."

But if all that were true (which I find hard to believe), then what are we to make of the rest of the passage? Just how are we to understand those strong commendations that Jesus gave to the Ephesians for the clarity of their gospel, their nobility of character, and their capacity for enduring hardship? Can anyone seriously maintain that these attributes imply a loss of love for the Savior?

Well, since I cannot learn what the passage means from those who might be expected to know, I shall speculate. Would you care to hear what I think was the "first love" that Jesus said the church at Ephesus had neglected? I think it was their love for each other.

Now, that may sound like one more assault on the inspired Word, a modern attempt to undercut the spiritual character of the gospel. It is not. Rather, it is a conclusion I derived explicitly from the Word of God. All through the Gospels, and in fact all through the New Testament, Christians are commanded to love each other. No other note is sounded so consistently. It is so clear that even unbelievers who choose never to go near a church, understand that to be a Christian is supposedly to be a loving kind of person. The tragedy is that the church today has so often overlooked what the world considers its prime mission, or else it has preferred to argue about it. We simply forget to love.

In our worship services we sing feelingly about our love for Jesus. Hundreds of new choruses are being composed on that theme. I enjoy singing them because my love

for Christ is what keeps me going. Most Christians understand that the vertical relationship is what determines the
horizontal.

We sing also about God's love, and how it embraces
the whole world. That takes care of another dimension. But
what about the base of the triangle? What about our love
for each other? We don't find many hymns in the hymnbook
about that. There's a line in Henry Van Dyke's "Joyful,
Joyful We Adore Thee" that reads, "Teach us how to love
each other." There is an old Negro song in which the following words appear:

> "Do you love everybody?"
> "Certainly, Lord.
> "Certainly, certainly, certainly, Lord."

There are a few other Christian songs about
brotherly love, but my guess is that the subject of mutual,
reciprocal love among human beings does not dominate the
hymnology of Christendom. The apostle John wrote,
"Beloved, if God so loved us, we ought also to love one
another,"[1] but I know a lot of Christians who apparently
never made that connection. A choir director in South
Dakota told me that he loved God so much he was ready to
choke anyone who said a word against Him. I have known
churchgoers who always arranged to leave the service by
the side door "so they wouldn't have to shake hands with
that man back there."

Something is missing! And when we study the New
Testament we discover that the love element was frequently missing in the early church as well. The Third Letter of
John leaves no doubt about that. My conclusion is that a
large part of the New Testament was written primarily to
complete the triangle; that is, to get Christians to love each
other.

Not to get people to love Jesus! Remember, much of

this scriptural compilation was addressed to Christian congregations, to people who already loved Jesus. And it was not written primarily to tell people that Jesus loved them. They already knew that. Nor was it written to reveal to them God's great love affair with the human race; they knew about that too.

Actually only a small part of the New Testament was directed to sinners, for the purpose of rescuing them from the brink of hell. Certainly these books were not composed to save the human race, or to lift the moral tone, or to weave the social fabric, or to establish rules for civilized living, or to promote the spread of the church. Nothing like that!

The New Testament was written to let people know "that Jesus is the Christ, the Son of God, and that by believing [they might] have life in his name."[2] But it was also written to get Christians into a loving relationship with each other. Jesus knew that until and unless that happened, nothing would happen; but once it did begin to occur, the kingdom of God would become a reality. That is why He said, "Seek first the kingdom, and all these things will be added to you."[3] The kingdom? What was the kingdom? God's kingdom of love, what else?

That is why we need the Holy Spirit poured into our hearts. To be filled with the Spirit is to be filled with love; and once we are filled, we have all the equipment we need to go out and win the world to Christ. For what is evangelism? It is people loving people into the circle of God's love.

Look with me once more at the first few verses of Revelation 2. In verse 5 we read, "Remember that you have fallen, and repent, and do the first works; but if not, I am coming to you quickly, and I will remove your lampstand out of its place . . . " How are we to interpret this symbolism? According to the time-honored practice, by comparing Scripture with Scripture. The lampstand's obvious function is to give light. In 1 John 1:5-7 are found the words, "God is light . . . If we should say that we have fellowship with him, and walk in darkness, we lie . . . If we walk in the light as He is in the light, we have fellowship with one another." In 1 John 2:9-10 appears the same symbolism: "He that says he is in the light, and hates his brother, is in the darkness . . . He that loves his brother dwells in the light."

The conclusion is inescapable: In these passages at least, light and love are the same thing. The lampstand is the symbol of our love for each other. And since the Holy Spirit is love, the church that does not reflect the love of God within its membership finds that the Holy Spirit has departed. He tiptoed out the center aisle and put a sign, *ICHABOD,* over the lintel of the door.[4] And He took the lampstand with Him.

Take your own survey of church members in your acquaintance. Ask each one how he or she happened to join the church fellowship to which they now belong. Most will tell you that they came because someone loved them. Far more important than the preacher, the music, the convenience of location, or even the doctrine, was the warmth of love they felt. They were looking for love and they found it. But to tell the truth, everybody is looking for love. Some are looking in the wrong places. Whether the church is the right place does not depend on outer appearance or appointments; it depends first of all on the inner life of us who believe — that is, the people they meet when they walk through the church door.

Each of us, I keep suggesting, can have a private castle, where we meet with our Lord. In that castle is a chapel, and on a table in that chapel, near the cross, is a lamp. As long as we love each other, that lamp is burning. Why don't you take a look right now?

Chapter Six

See if it is even there!

PRAYER

Savior and Redeemer, holy Lord, put me through this chapter again. I need to get on track. I don't want to be filled with everything else; I want to be filled with Your Holy Spirit. Don't write *ICHABOD* [the glory is departed] over me yet. Give me time; I need to lay aside a few more weights before Christ can be formed in me.

S·E·V·E·N

How do we guard our minds against the intrusions that soil our thoughts and—worst of all—waste our time?

THE
GREAT
DISTRACTION

I throw myself down in my chamber, and I invite God and His angels thither, and when they are there, I neglect God and His angels for the noise of a fly, for the rattling of a coach, for the whining of a door.
—John Donne

Of all the obstacles to the productive inner life of a dedicated believer, distraction ranks as Public Enemy Number One. Thoughts of God can be whisked away by an earthquake shaking the house, a dancer performing on the TV screen, or a ladybug crawling on the window pane. A preacher friend of mine chained himself to the leg of his bed so he would not be diverted from spending an hour in prayer. Unfortunately there is no chain that will keep the mind from wandering away from its contemplation of truth, goodness and beauty.

We may as well admit that the problem affects us all. We want to be pure in heart; we want to keep our eyes fixed on Jesus; we want desperately to keep evil thoughts from taking over our private castle and polluting our thought processes; but when temptation comes, all too often we succumb. Then, disgusted with ourselves, we wrench away from the sordid topic that was distracting us and try to get on with our Christian life.

I am not dealing now with overt distractions, such as deliberately seeking out dubious company, or picking up a rotten book. Rather I am attempting to describe the tempting and unprofitable mental images that occupy so much of our thinking. How do we handle them? E. Stanley Jones once remarked that he did it simply by batting his eyes. That enabled him to switch over to a more profitable area of contemplation. I have a feeling, however, that it wouldn't take long for temptation to circumvent that technique.

The place to start, perhaps, is with Jesus Himself. He was, as the Letter to the Hebrews reminds us, "tempted in every way, just as we are."[1] Yet He also was, to quote Dr. Trevor Davies, "a perfectly adjusted moral personality, with all the mighty endowment of His instinctive nature under control."[2] To be like Jesus in our inner life is what the Christian life is all about. We want that control. How do we get it? How do we guard our minds against the intrusions that soil our thoughts and—worst of all—waste our time?

We shall take on four of these time-wasters in order clearly to identify the enemy.

Anger

The first is anger. Right now we are angry. An individual, a group, a company is on our list, and we would like to blow them away. We spend hours plotting revenge. It becomes an obsession. It eats us alive. "Some day!" we say. What fools we are! Vengeance is probably the theme of 90 percent of television crime shows. It has inspired more ugly thoughts, and motivated more useless behavior, than any other incentive known to the human race. And it always makes things worse for us than they were before. "Don't get mad, get even," reads the bumper sticker. But you never get even, because when you do, you attempt to justify your action and that makes you more bitter than ever, and you carry your bitterness with you to the grave. Some inner life! But it gets even worse, for after death you face the Judgment and learn the truth at last: "Vengeance is mine, I will repay, says the Lord."[3]

Fear

The second great distracter is fear. It comes to us during the dark patches of the night, a gnawing dread of something or other that upsets us. We lie awake anticipating the worst that could happen. We repeat the 23rd Psalm, the Lord's Prayer, and any other Scriptures that come to mind, but the words we know by rote have little effect on the agitations of our heart. A burglar, a fire, a dam bursting, an earthquake, a tornado, an accident, a pregnancy, a stock market collapse, an invasion, a nuclear explosion, whatever it is we imagine or anticipate, it brings one supreme reaction—FEAR!

When the limbs are trembling, the skin is crawling, and the eyes are dilating, it is rather specious to talk about a buoyant inner life. One does not concentrate easily on God while sitting on the panic button.

Greed

A third deterrent to peace of mind is greed, sometimes known as covetousness. It is well known in the work place that when a laborer is thinking only about money, he derives no joy from his work, and his output suffers. The morbid fixation to accumulate is a terrible sickness; it twists the mental processes and destroys interpersonal relationships. By contrast, the inner life of the believer is contingent upon the believer's state of contentment; and one can learn to be content, as the apostle Paul reminded us, with very little.

It is hard to be cheated out of what rightfully belongs to us. But it is even worse to be cheated out of a victorious, Spirit-filled, contented state of being by a financial deal that went sour. History teaches us that many a revival of genuine Christian faith in America took place after the bottom dropped out of the market. As the old gospel song put it,

> Far better than gold
> and wealth untold
> are the riches of love in Christ Jesus.

Lust

Lust is the last of the distracters we shall consider, and in many ways it is the most insidious. It packs a wallop that can put the others to shame. It creeps into our thinking almost without our knowing it. It eats up time as though there were nothing else in life.

Not everyone is affected by it. There are those who are celibate by choice; our Lord Himself, according to the record, was one of them. But many are living celibate lives today simply because nothing else is open to them. They would like to be "delivered" if the way were clear. Others have known the fulfillment of marriage, but for one reason or another are now celibate. They may have since tried some kind of relationship, in an attempt to deal with the problem of lust, but have found it unsatisfactory.

Still others continue in marriage, but to say they have found fulfillment in it would be an overstatement. Like Sinclair Lewis' Babbitt, they dream of something they don't have, something fairy-like, elusive and tantalizing that manages to take up hours of their time and produces precisely nothing. This is the total content of their inner life: a hollow vacuum of thwarted lust that is eagerly exploited by the sex merchants, but yields only frustration and despair.

For those who desire the celibate life, sexual temptation is no hindrance to the development of a healthy inner life. For the rest of us, a happy, fulfilling marriage is the best prospect. Promiscuity, homosexuality, live-in relationships can only aggravate the problem. Indulged in, they sooner or later destroy the peace of mind needed to communicate with our God and to walk humbly with Him.

But how do we get rid of these time-wasting monsters—anger, fear, greed and lust? How do we get to that bourne of security where the world does not bother us; where our daily actions are hid with Christ in God, and where we can look out at life with steady eyes?

Let me try another approach. For once, instead of using religious language, let me quote from a noted psychologist, Carl Gustav Jung: "No inferior form of energy can be simply converted into a superior form unless at the same time a source of higher value lends it support."[4] In other words, we don't get more from less unless something new is added.

That source of higher value, that "something new" is in this case the Holy Spirit. He invades the thinking process of the believer and suffuses it with love. This love, poured into the believer's soul, brings about three possible outlets for the mind that is beset by troubling thoughts. One is anticipation, one is relaxation, and one is sublimation.

Chapter Seven

Anticipation

Anticipation is an excellent deterrent to thinking in wrong directions because it concentrates on good things that are going to happen. The return of Christ, the assurance of heaven, the glory of entering the throne room of the Most High, of seeing God face to face, of being reunited with loved ones—these are the promises that thrill the heart of the believer; alongside them the attractions of this world lose much of their luster.

Anticipation is not however completely wrapped up in the climax of history. This life is not without its blessings, and in the providence of God the Spirit-filled believer will find abundant evidence that God's mercies are "new every morning." There is always something to praise God about; always something to make the heart sing even in the direst straits. Just ahead God is preparing for those who love Him some kind of feast, some special boon, that keeps the Christian life from ever becoming stale. Thinking about it is a prime alternative to temptation.

Relaxation

Another outlet for the mind is simply relaxation. We do something to divert the tendency to daydream or fantasize. We pick up the telephone, or read a book, or play a game, or engage in strenuous exercise. Nothing is more therapeutic to the soul than simply taking a walk. I like to climb a rocky hill that presents some difficulty. As I sort out the best way to attack the summit, I find myself so absorbed that my mind is set free from all the things that were clamoring for its attention.

Relaxation with Christian friends is an uplifting antidote to all forms of temptation. We respond to a positive environment that brings out the best in us. To relate stories, to laugh, to let the refreshing presence of good and lovable people clear away the cobwebs, is better than any number of cold showers!

One of the best aids to the inner life of a believer is a happy marriage. As I walked past a television screen recently I overheard a woman asking, "Is a monogamous relationship possible?" What a world we have made for ourselves! We have dug a pit and have fallen into it. Not only is monogamy possible, it is the only relationship between man and woman that works. If the media only knew it, millions of people around the world can testify that marital happiness is God's best gift to the human race. It is the one ongoing reality that tops them all.

A joy-filled marriage reduces the time spent in distracting and useless thoughts to something like zero. The Christian husband and wife who have found fulfillment and pleasure in matrimony can turn to God as easily as to each other. When they hold hands in prayer, it seems to them that they are also holding God's hand; and the inner life glows with a new radiance.

Whether or not a person is happily married, the chief end of human life remains, in the words of the old catechism, "to glorify God and enjoy Him forever." We are to put ourselves on the line for Jesus Christ and spend our lives in morally valuable and socially useful efforts for Him. That kind of activity and lifestyle corrals the instinctive energy that God has planted in each of our bodies.

Sublimation

Within the human psyche there is a latent power or energy that often impedes the clarity of our thought, and sends us down sloughs and alleys of negative, time-wasting mental exercise. Psychologists have coined various names for it—instinct, drive, need, libido. Choose your own name; it is this energy that so often ambushes us outside the castle and keeps us away from our Lord. It has us chasing chimeras and hurting other people. It leads us into unfamiliar places and puts us in compromising situations. A lot of it is simply the unleashed expression of bodily appetites.

Many Christians have had trouble with this major distraction. To experiment with it is to violate biblical teaching and invite disaster. To repress it is psychologically dangerous. To attempt to ignore it is often to turn life into a giant bore. Millions of frustrated people are attempting just to "get through" the day or the week, and are looking for anything that will "entertain" them so that they won't have to think about what they have to "put up with." They watch the soap operas; they revel in scandals; they read trash, if they read anything; they have, in a word, traded life for existence.

God, however, has not left those who believe in Himself in this desolate state. He always makes provision for His own. As the apostle Paul says, He has left us a way of escape. Millions of Christians have found ways to put their strong instinctive drives to work to make the earth a more beautiful and livable place. They have harnessed their bodily energy and placed it at the service of others.

Students of human behavior call this activity "sublimation." The word sublimation has some technical overtones, but popularly it is used to describe the efforts people make to re-direct their natural energies and put them to use in socially beneficial and morally valuable ways. Instinctive drives, which if given free rein would invite self-destruction and social chaos, become transmuted into expressions of love.[6] The father who loses his only son launches a ministry that provides shelter and training for hundreds of homeless youth. The disappointed lover devotes his life to medical research and makes a discovery that relieves suffering for millions. The poet, handicapped by physical deformity (as was Alexander Pope) or frustrated by an incompatible marriage (as was T. S. Eliot) thrills the world with his genius.

In the summer of 1985 my late wife's physician informed me that they had done all they could; her cancer was beyond surgical help.

"How long?" I asked him.

"Six months or six years."

That night I went to my knees as usual and prayed for her. Then I asked, "What about me?"

It was one of the few times I received a direct answer: "Put on the armor." Whatever I wanted to do with my life, it was to be subordinated to another's needs. For the next fifteen months I literally lived a different life. My "vital energies," along with everything else, were transmuted into a new lifestyle. When death came as God ordained, that special duty was terminated, but the blessing of caring for a loved one outlived the sorrow.

Many others, whose experiences went deeper than mine, have testified that sublimation can take all the pressures that life brings to bear, all the anger, fear, worry, covetousness, and lust, and the unfulfilled desires of a boxed-in career, and re-channel them into something that God will use to His glory. The sublimated life becomes irradiated by a tender, loving relationship with the living God. Ashes become beauty; mourning becomes the oil of joy; the spirit of heaviness becomes the garment of praise.

Once the believer has set his feet on this path, he is able by the grace of God to orient and guide the rampaging needs of the flesh toward a serene way of life that reaches out to others. Such a way of life has a retroactive effect; it yields satisfaction and gratification beyond imagining for the one who adopts it. The Bible calls it a "good conscience." The inner becomes the outer. The castle well becomes a fountain of good works.

Chapter Seven

God took my plate glass life
and shattered it
then gathered the broken pieces
and made them into windchimes.
— Glenda Palmer

PRAYER

Beloved Abba God, who created and invented time
for Your creatures to use, keep me from wasting it. Show
me how to redeem the waking hours by avoiding the
temptations that beset me. Give me a sense of timing
that locks into Your perfect will. I pray through Him who
was Himself the Fullness of time.

*Until we pray with and for someone else, or
have been prayed for ourselves, we don't
discover that prayer is God's tool
to teach us how to love.*

THE OTHER KIND OF PRAYER

He...made intercession for the transgressors.
—Isaiah 53:12

We have worked our way through a maze of distractions and hindrances to the achievement of a quiet inner life. We have discovered that the main roadblock is a lack of love for each other. Now we are down to our basic subject. We are ready for the T-bone steak and baked potatoes of life in the castle of our soul. In a word, we are ready for prayer.

What is prayer?

Let us look at some definitions and descriptions:

"Prayer is the soul's sincere desire . . . " (James Montgomery).

"Prayer is the world in tune" (Henry Vaughan).

"Prayer is lying in the sunshine of God's grace" (Ole Hallesby).

"Prayer is for life what original research is for science — by it we get direct contact with reality" (P. T. Forsyth).

"No individual is greater than his prayer life" (Leonard Ravenhill).

"The person who kneels to God can stand up to anything" (Louis Evans, Sr.).

"Prayer does not enable us to do a greater work for God. Prayer *is* a greater work for God" (Thomas Chalmers).

"There is not in the world a kind of love more sweet and delightful than a continual conversation with God" (Brother Lawrence).

"Many a fellow is praying for rain with his tub the wrong side up" (Samuel Porter Jones).

"I like ejaculatory prayer; it reaches heaven before the devil can get a shot at it" (Rowland Hill).

"If your knees are knocking, kneel on them" (from the wall of a London air raid shelter).[1]

Without prayer there is no inner life, whether we are believers or not: for prayer *is* the inner life. Were all the Bibles in the world to be destroyed, together with all the devotional books, hymnbooks, and theological volumes, and all sermons on tape or film, and all church buildings and church schools and colleges, and all Christian radio and television towers, until every vestige of Christianity had been wiped from the earth, for millions of people the life of prayer would go on unhindered. After awhile the books and facilities would be replaced; but the relationship between a human being and the Creator would be uninterrupted. For prayer is like breathing; it is the inhaling and exhaling

72

of the soul. Since the time of our first parents, it has been the lifeline of communication between the human creature and its Maker.

Why do believers pray? Basically, because we feel so helpless. There is a great gulf fixed between what we have and what we want, and there seems no way across it. Our human resources are soon exhausted. "I have been driven to my knees many times," said Abraham Lincoln, "by the overwhelming conviction that I had nowhere else to go." It was a very simple motive that started young Augustine praying, as he tells us in his *Confessions*: "We [boys] found men praying to you; and we learned from them . . . to think of you as some great being who . . . was able to hear us and help us. So as a boy I too began praying to you . . . I begged . . . that I might not be whipped at school."[2]

Such is the usual agenda when people pray. Let's say right now you have a need; you find yourself unable to meet that need; you exhaust every channel, every resource, and are finally driven to seek help from God Himself. You are encouraged in your Bible reading to do this, and now you are delighted, even amazed, to find that your prayers are answered in ways beyond your imagining. Your faith in the living God is strengthened; your love for Christ, who taught us to pray, is deepened; and it would seem that your inner life is in magnificent shape.

Watch out! Beware!

To be pulled out of a pit when we thought we were stuck there forever is a thrill that taxes the imagination. But what happens to us personally is certainly not the whole point of prayer. We may be missing the best part, and losing out on the choicest blessing.

Go back with me briefly to the early 1940s. I was a student in a liberal theological seminary, taking a required course in what was called religious education. It was a "methods" course, based on the philosophy of John Dewey.[3] The subject of the lectures was prayer. We were told that prayer consists of five parts: adoration, confession, thanksgiving, supplication and submission; the acronym being ACTSS. It has taken me many years to conclude that while ACTSS may be an ingenious teaching tool, it has limitations in coming to grips with God in direct communication; furthermore, it omits the one aspect of prayer that in recent years has revolutionized my own devotional life. That word is intercession.

Jesus taught us to pray for the coming of His kingdom, not only that it would come for us personally, but would come for others as well. In Isaiah 59 God "wondered that there was no intercessor."[4] In 1 Timothy the apostle Paul called for intercession by Christians.[5] Again and again the Bible commands us to pray for others, not just in a general way, but specifically. We are to get on "praying ground," as the phrase goes, not just to satisfy our own clamoring wants, but also the wants and needs of those around us. We are to be intercessors.

Right here, it would seem, is the way out of many of our difficulties associated with prayer. We admit privately that prayer bores us. It never bores us when we are with someone else, our hand on his, our lips praying for him. We complain that our thoughts are distracted and we can't concentrate. That never happens when we are interceding for a friend in his presence. We argue that prayer is a waste of time because it doesn't do anything; specifically that it makes no difference in our situation. That point is hard to maintain when the person for whom we have prayed assures us in so many words that our prayer made a tremendous difference in his or her life.

Prayer is actually a vehicle of love. It is God's tool to teach us how to love. But until we pray with and for someone else, or have been prayed for ourselves, we don't discover that. Life gives us many exciting moments, but I know of no thrill to match that of being the object of someone else's prayers, especially if the prayer is offered in my hearing, with a hand on my shoulder. It almost seems as if God takes special notice of prayers when they are offered for someone else.

I first learned about intercession in 1954 through reading Norman Grubb's remarkable book, *Rees Howells, Intercessor*, the story of a Welsh coal miner who founded a Bible school.[6] For some time I had known that no one can lead another closer to Christ than he stands himself. Now I found the same principle applying to intercession: "One only asks God to do through another what he is willing for the Lord to do through him . . . The Holy Spirit can never 'bind the strong man' through us on a higher level than that in which He has first had victory in us."

At one point I found Rees Howells left me behind. He spoke frequently of "gaining an abiding place of intercession," some kind of spiritual position that enabled him to enter into "the grace of faith." From this position he was able to pray for others and watch God bring victory, even when his own personal prayers were not answered as he had hoped.

I have found no such abiding place. I am right down with everyone else. My private castle gives me no special leverage with God. It is not a place to "charge my spiritual batteries"; it is not a castle of power but of love. The Holy Spirit is love. He meets me in love. To claim anything else would be for me to go the way of all flesh, and I would start boasting again.

It would be great to trumpet about my personal spiritual victories through prayer, but you are reading the wrong author. I do talk to God on my knees and in the silent stretches of the night, but to call me a man of prayer would be like calling Baron von Munchhausen the paragon of veracity. Heaven shakes its head over my personal devotions; and yet I will cross two state lines to pray with and for somebody else.

Make no mistake, intercession is not just a friendly gesture of encouragement, or a psychological exercise, or a means of relieving tension, or a conversation with one's "higher self." In intercession we expect answers! We find that among Christians there is no such thing as unanswered prayer. (Let's rewrite that hymn verse, "Teach me the patience of unanswered prayer"; it sounds as if only the lucky ones get the answers.) God always answers the prayers of believers. He does so in one of three ways: He says "Yes," He says "No" or He says "Wait." (Waiting is the subject of the next chapter.) The "Yes" comes when we ask according to His sovereign will. If He says "Yes" it is because the prayer is an honorable one; it honors Himself, who is Love. Sometimes it is His own prayer. If He answers "No" it may be because the prayer, like so many we offer, can really be answered best by ourselves, and thus it is not worthy of divine attention. Or it may have other flaws. Someone has remarked that most prayers can be answered either by a gift of money or a kind friend.

And then there are the prayers that are simply mean! I find it hard to believe that God rewards invectives, curses and maledictions. It is true that people have from time immemorial besought their Lord to send wrath and judgment on their enemies, as well as on evildoers of all kinds. What this contributes to the inner life of the believer is beyond me. God is love. The Holy Spirit is love. Jesus taught us to love our enemies. Prayer is God's instrument to teach us to love; it is not a device for getting back at those whose behavior we do not like. God knows all about evildoers. He does not need us to advise Him as to what to do about them. He is the Judge.

Prayer teaches us to love God; intercessory prayer teaches us to love each other. The first Quaker, George Fox, said, "I have prayed to be baptized into a sense of all conditions, that I might be able to know the needs and feel the sorrows of all."[7] And William Law wrote three hundred years ago, "I have proved from actual firsthand experience that is impossible to harbor ill will and animosity against anyone if you keep praying for him. There is nothing that makes us love a man so much as praying for him."[8]

Arthur John Gossip, whom I once heard preach in Edinburgh, Scotland, has a marvelous chapter in *In the Secret Place of the Most High* on "the priestly office of a Christian," which he says is intercession.[9] He explains: "In the prayer of intercession we are given the chance to exercise our high office and prerogative, the priesthood of believers, to help Christ in His healing and saving of this vast needy world." He says that intercessory prayer is the

---

Young Billy Graham rose from his seat, walked to the front and knelt on the oak floor.

---

most spontaneous and natural kind of praying; and that "if you keep praying for the people about you, you will find yourself a happier person, set in a world that has surely grown friendlier."

Dr. Gossip tells us that when Ulrich Zwingli set out to reform the worship of the Swiss churches in 1525, he opened and closed each service with an intercessory prayer. He explained the change by saying that Christ's law of love makes us think first of others. (Apparently Zwingli had an ancient precedent; some eastern churches of the fourth century followed the same worship pattern.)

This is a book about the believer's inner life, not about the prayer life of our churches. But I may be pardoned if I digress long enough to say that if we forget to pray for others in our personal devotions, we show the same forgetfulness in our evangelical churches. Intercession is an ecclesiastical lost art. If we do bring others before God, asking Him to help them, the prayers are often so vague and general that I sometimes imagine the heavenly Father reacting as He did to the Israelites: "When you make many prayers, I will not hear!"[10]

The worship leader in our typical church service does make an effort to offer a general prayer, whose pattern might be thus:

"We pray for the President, the Vice-President, the Congress, the Governor, the Mayor, the City Council, the fire department, the police department, the sanitation department, the men and women in the armed forces, the missionaries, the young people on retreat at Camp Dripping Willows, the sick, the people in hospitals, the prisoners in our jails."

I have even heard of a minister who prayed for the people who were still at home trying to make up their minds whether to come to church.

The tragedy is that in all this intercession, no mention was made of the people who were already in church, and who had come presumably because they felt the need to be prayed for. Should we then dispense with public intercession? Of course not. Scripture commands it. Let's have more of it! But let the prayers cover all the bases and not stay forever out in left field.

Let me tell you about an intercessory prayer meeting that God answered in a most remarkable way. It took place on the night of Wednesday, July 13, 1949, in a room of the Westminster Hotel in Winona Lake, Indiana, during an early convention of Youth for Christ. It began at 10 P.M. and went on for six hours, after a full day of meetings. The time was spent praying, singing, quoting Bible verses and praising the Lord.

At 3 A.M. in the morning Armin Gesswein, the convention's prayer chairman, stood to his feet. "Fellows," he said, "our brother Billy Graham is going to Los Angeles for a crusade in a few weeks. Why don't we just gather around and lay our hands on him and ask God for a fresh touch to anoint him for this work?"

Young Billy Graham rose from his seat, walked to the front and knelt on the oak floor. A dozen men joined him. Hands were laid on and the intercession began. When it was over and the men were still kneeling, Billy opened his Bible to Joel 3:13-14 and began to read: "Put ye in the sickle, for the harvest is ripe: come, get you down, for the press is full, the fats overflow; for their wickedness is great. Multitudes, multitudes in the valley of decision: for the day of the Lord is near in the valley of decision."

Then Billy said, "That's the verse I am taking with me to the West Coast. I believe if we will put in the sickle, we shall reap an unprecedented harvest of souls for Christ."

The following month, in a tent at the corner of Washington Boulevard and Hill street, Los Angeles, the crusade began that launched Billy Graham and his team on an incredible worldwide ministry which continues unabated to this day. Millions who were wandering aimlessly in the valley of decision have decided for Jesus Christ.

I can add a personal footnote. In the fall of 1957 I was pastoring a church across the Bay from San Francisco when the news came that Billy Graham might be coming for an evangelistic crusade. The matter was still in doubt; Billy had injured his leg. I felt a strong desire to pray all night for him and for this event—something I had never done. A friend who directed San Francisco's Youth for Christ rally also wanted to spend a night in prayer, and prevailed on his brother-in-law, who served a small church in Hayward, to join us. We arrived at his church at 11 P.M. and spent the night praying for each other's needs—and for Billy. It was a most exhilarating experience. We prayed, we sang, we read Scripture, we wept, we lifted up not only Billy but his team, the churches, San Francisco, the whole Bay Area—until dawn.

In April, 1958, the Graham team arrived and stayed seven weeks, holding services every night in the Cow Palace. It was a wonderful crusade; God answered our prayers beyond all expectation. Every city surrounding the Bay was touched as thousands of men, women and young people joined the family of God through commitment to Jesus Christ. And may I add, one small development occurred that had never been anticipated or dreamed of in our long night of prayer several months before. When Billy left San Francisco, he took me with him.

Often, when a believer finally gets down to serious praying, intercession is not foremost in his thoughts. He is wrestling with a weighty personal problem, a vital, intimate matter, and is desperate for relief. Subjective and introspective prayers make up a large portion of the Christian life, and without them God would seem remote indeed. God forbid that I should minimize their value or importance. Whether they bring the fruits of joy and blessing, you can judge as well as I. My aim is simply to point out that the benefits of prayer are much more in evidence, and easier to feel, when we put our personal petitions aside, get out of ourselves and begin praying for others.

A husband is about to go out the front door. His wife comes for a good-bye kiss, then touches his arm and says a brief prayer for him. A schoolboy is about to engage in a game. His brother stops and prays for him. A girl student faces a difficult examination. Her boyfriend lifts her up to God. A jurist is about to enter his courtroom. The telephone rings in his chambers. A friend is on the line, wanting to pray for him.

Intercession! It is one of life's greatest enrichments.

I will never be a giant of prayer. I don't care for the title. Let someone else climb on a pillar like Simeon Stylites. Let someone else compose beautiful cadences for the prayer books. To each his own. What I want to do with my inner life is to get my own agenda sorted out before the Lord. Indeed, Rees Howells said it well: "One only asks God to do through another what he is willing for the Lord to do through him." And then I would like to cultivate a greater sensitivity to the heart cries of my fellow human beings, whether in or out of church. If I succeed, perhaps the Lord will put me close enough to them to pray with them.

PRAYER

O Heart of all Loveliness and Beauty, since my speech is not fluent in public, teach me to open up freely in my conversation with You when we are alone together. Help me to keep my personal requests in line with Your will, and let my intercession for others work mightily, for Jesus Christ's sake I pray. Amen.

N·I·N·E

Why does God make us wait? "Yes" is beautiful; "No" we can live with; but "Wait" is a drag. Why does He put us through it?

WHEN GOD SAYS 'WAIT'

Be strong and take heart and wait for the Lord.
—Psalm 27:14 (NIV)

You are a knight-errant riding up to the castle where your King is residing. You have been on important assignment for Him, and you come bearing a particular request that will have a direct effect on your future movements. It is essential that you not only are granted an audience, but that your petition be acted upon with royal favor. From the watchtower yeomen have observed your approach. You rein up before the drawbridge without dismounting, expecting the bridge to be lowered so you can cross over the moat and enter the bailey. Your steed paws the ground impatiently.

From behind the castle a young varlet comes running toward you. He reaches up and hands you a note. You open it and read: "His Majesty is delighted that you have come, but sends His regrets that He cannot just at this time act on the purpose of your embassage. He requests that you kindly wait." The varlet disappears. The draw-bridge remains up.

Nothing can cause the inner life of a believer to flourish like a prompt answer to prayer. We ask God for something and He delivers it. We decide God is real, is personally interested in our welfare, is kind and loving and altogether marvelous. We exult in the gracious favor of our Lord.

But sometimes the response is put on the spindle. We ask God to do it, we think He should do it, we expect Him to do it, we put out fleeces and rearrange our plans in the belief that He will do it, but time passes and nothing happens. We can't seem to get any clear word. Our inner life is still intact, we haven't given up our faith, but over our relationship with God there hangs a giant question mark. We wonder if the answer is "No." That being the case, why doesn't God say so right out? The delay is exasperating, and the longer it lasts, the more confusing life becomes. Milton wrote, "They also serve who only stand and wait,"[1] but how long is the waiting expected to go on? How long before the drawbridge is lowered?

In an effort to address the problem, I have prepared a dialogue between a young Christian, not too well grounded, and his heavenly Father. It is not intended to be taken too seriously, from a theological perspective; but it does seek to illustrate why God does not respond with alacrity to some of our batterings on the heavenly gates. I will have a final comment at the close.

Well, Father.
Yes, son.

I thought I'd better check in with You. I'm kind of waiting for an answer.

From me?

Who else? I mean, that's it, isn't it? If You say go...

What do you want?

I want to be filled with Your Spirit.

Are you sure of this?

You bet. I want it all—the baptism, the anointing, the indwelling, the gifts, the fruit, the whole package.

And?

Well, it's like the ball is in Your court, sort of. Everything's set.

How is everything set?

Well, You know. I prayed and humbled myself.

How did you humble yourself?

Well, I thought I did. And I fasted.

One meal.

Look, Father, I'm serious. I'm waiting on You.

And I am waiting on you.

Do You have to? After all, You made me. You know I'm young and full of life. I want to see some action. I've watched what happens when You pour Your Spirit into some other guys. It's really neat. I can't wait to get in on it.

So you can't wait.

No. Why should I? What's the point of waiting? I don't have forever, Lord.

But I do.

That's fine for You, Father. What about the people who are dying every day and going to hell?

You have plans?

85

Big plans, Father. I mean, I've got commitments You wouldn't believe. Programs, schedules, contacts, you name it. We're going everywhere: Patagonia, Bessarabia, Sikkim, Kamchatka . . .

Then why are you here?

I thought I explained that. I want to be filled with Your Spirit. I'm no dummy. I know I need help.

Yes, you do.

You gave me the power once. When I was saved, I was so wound up, I felt I could do anything.

What happened?

I guess I ran out of gas. Who knows? Maybe my ego went on a trip.

True.

But that's all cleared up now. I checked myself out.

Well!

So here I am.

Yes.

Father, look, I think You're putting me on.

Why?

You're stalling.

No. You are stalling.

I'm waiting to be filled with Your Spirit. Otherwise I can't make it. You know that.

Then wait, my son.

But how long?

Simeon waited.

Who?

Simeon.

That old dude in the temple when they brought the

baby Jesus?

Yes.

But he waited all his life.

That's right.

I give up.

Jacob waited. Hannah waited. David waited.

What are You telling me?

There were people waiting for Pentecost in the upper room.

Timing. I get it. You're giving me some logistics about timing.

Refuseniks are waiting right now in the Soviet Union.

True. They're building support. You want me to do that? Build up support while I wait?

You have not even begun to wait.

Begun? It seems as if I've been here for days.

But you have not been waiting.

What have I been doing?

Fidgeting. Squirming. Complaining. Telling me how busy and important you are.

All right, I'll quit. I'll just shut my eyes and go limp.

Fine.

I'll probably go to sleep.

Excellent.

I don't have to remind you that the devil isn't asleep, Father. He is tearing up the place. If You ask me, he has taken over and is about to finish off the human race.

Do you wish to engage him in combat?

No. I want to be filled with Your Spirit so that You

will engage him in combat. I know I can't take him on alone.
So we had better get on with it, don't You think? It isn't
that I mind waiting, You understand. I just don't have the
aptitudes for it.

Get on with what?

Father, if You're going to do something in me, do it.

What do you wish done?

Give me a fresh touch of the Holy Spirit like You
gave the other guys. I don't know what it is. Just rev me
up. Set me going.

Do you wish the fire, too?

Fire? What fire? I don't understand.

You are talking to me, son, not to room service.

I know, Father, believe me, I know. You are om-
nipotent, omniscient, immortal, immutable, all-wise,
all-knowing, all-glorious, the Sovereign Majesty, the
Creator of the heavens and the earth. But You are also my
Father, and You told us to make our requests known to
You, didn't You?

Make your requests.

You sound as if I don't have any rights with You.

You have the right to call me Father.

And I have the right to ask You something?

*You do. But your rights are not Crown rights. I move
at my good pleasure.*

Where does that leave me?

State your problem, son.

OK, once more. I want to be filled with Your Spirit
because my tank has gone dry.

Oh, no, it has not.

You mean there's some fuel in the bottom?

Too much.

How can I empty it?

By my Spirit.

But when? When? When?

Wait.

Obviously the young man needs more discipling before he can be filled with anything but himself. Even so, the question he raises about waiting on God will not lie down. Over the centuries some of the world's greatest minds have wrestled with it. Why does God make us wait? Why does He make the heavens seem like brass? "Yes" is beautiful; "No" we can live with, even if we don't like it; but "Wait" is a drag. Why does He put us through it?

I have listened to many voices on this matter, and some have been helpful. Let me distill for you three observations that have come to me.

The first concerns timing. Since God invented time, He makes full use of it. The science of astronomy alone is ample witness to the truth that God's timing is perfect. To the person who is waiting on God, however, there is a word in the Greek New Testament that tells us even more about God's timing than do the books of astronomy. That word is *kairos,* which can be translated, *opportune* or *seasonable time.*[2] I know of no more exciting Bible study than an examination of that word as it appears throughout the New Testament. The inevitable conclusion is that when we are waiting on God, and become locked into God's timing, things begin to happen beyond all our hopes and imaginings.

The second observation is that God does not tell us to wait just to test our patience. He often delays His answer so it will bring a greater blessing. A fascinating passage in Isaiah 30:18 indicates just that: "The Lord will wait, that he might be gracious to you." Charles Spurgeon once told his young pastors that whenever the Lord was preparing a larger blessing for his ministry, He first put him through a depression. As he expressed it, "The scouring of the vessel fitted it for the Master's use."[3] By waiting, God makes His answer to the believer's prayer all the more glorious and complete. The result is that our cups run over.

My third observation is that when the wait is over, we sometimes find that the answer came in a form different from what we expected. We got not what we wanted so much as what we needed; or perhaps what we wanted for ourselves was given to someone near and dear to us. God has many ways of ending the waiting. Charles Williams, the English author, once wrote, "Usually the way must be made for heaven, and then it will come by some other; the sacrifice must be made ready, and the fire will strike on another altar."[4] That is because God is free. His ways are not our ways. We must never forget that He moves according to the sublimity of His own desire, which may or may not be our own heart's desire. So often what He wants for us is so much better than what we had written down on our own prayer list.

The knight-errant was finally admitted through the castle gate, but it took longer than he anticipated. A riderless horse had come by, and the knight had ridden off in search of the missing rider. After several hours he found him lying unconscious by a stream, and took him to a nearby farmhouse where the man was revived. This, too, was in the good pleasure of the Father's will.

PRAYER

Great Listener to the Universe, since You ask that I wait on You, teach me to wait for the right things, and not impose on Your attention when I can solve the problem myself. But if You're holding back in order to bring a larger blessing, then, O Lover of my soul, hold me back, too. Amen.

T·E·N

If the inner life of the believer is to have any reality, the love of God has to be worked in.

WHAT IS THE INNER LIFE FOR?

If any man will do his will, he shall know of the doctrine.
—John 7:17

Thousands of people who consider themselves believers ("Naturally I believe in God—doesn't everyone?") have no inner life whatever. They have no idea of what such a life would be like, and no particular desire to look into it. They don't quite see how it would fit into their present schedules. Behind their indifference is an unspoken but insistent question: "What's in it for me?"

We have taken up a few questions of our own, such as, "What is the inner life like?" but we have not so far raised a very practical question: "What is it for?"

To find an answer we must look to Scripture. In Matthew 7:21 Jesus tells His disciples, "Not everyone who says to me, 'Lord, Lord,' will enter the kingdom of heaven, but only he who does the will of my Father who is in heaven." Superficially, that sounds like a put-down of the inner life. It is not. The four Gospels, if they do nothing else, stand witness to the radiant inner life of our Lord Himself.

When the believer is in communication with the One who made him, he may well use an expression such as "Lord, Lord!" Why not? What's wrong with it? Nothing, except that by itself, as Jesus points out, it is just that—an expression. As far as the kingdom of heaven is concerned, doing God's will is what matters. But then, the whole purpose of the inner life is to discover God's will and do it. We sit at the Master's feet and learn the meaning and purpose of our living on this planet; then we set about fulfilling that purpose. We come in order to go.

But what is God's will? That is the question that has baffled kings and philosophers, billionaires and welfare recipients, and more importantly, you and me. Again and again, in the Old and New Testaments, people were hung up on the question: "Is it God's will to do this? Or should I do the other? Can I be certain that I have His approval and blessing? What about a sign from Him one way or another?"

Trying to get a handle on the future has always been a major human occupation. People have tried crystal gazing, trance speaking, palmistry, casting lots, inspecting entrails, listening to shells, astrology, reading footprints in ashes, watching flights of birds, and dream interpretation. The kings of ancient Greece would sail to Delphi, bringing their costly gifts to the oracle, seeking from the pythoness of Apollo an answer to the same old question: "Should I or shouldn't I?"

Today people are looking for God's will in much the same spirit. I'm not sure whether President John Kennedy prayed for enlightenment before he sent the anti-Castro Cubans into the Bay of Pigs. Many people, faced with such a decision, would cast about for an omen. They would flip a coin, or watch for a lucky number. Others frankly seek God's will. President Eisenhower told me that in 1943 he prayed God would favor his paratroopers during their invasion of Sicily. In Stephen Vincent Benét's epic poem about the Civil War, *John Brown's Body,* President Lincoln sits in the Oval Office and utters an eloquent complaint:

> They come to me and talk about God's will . . .
> Day after day . . .
>   . . . all of them are sure they know God's will.
> I am the only man who does not know it.
> And yet, if it is probable that God
> Should, and so very clearly, state His will
> To others, on a point of my own duty,
> It might be thought He would reveal it me
> Directly, more especially as I
> So earnestly desire to know His will.[1]

If the premise of these chapters is correct, Scripture gives a clear answer to the question, "What is God's will?" It is His will that believers in Him be filled with His Spirit. John the Baptist said as much when he prophesied that when the Messiah appeared, He would baptize with the Holy Spirit and with fire. Jesus Himself made it plain in His discourses in John 14–16. The apostle Paul capped it in his letter to the Ephesians when he wrote, "Be filled with the Spirit."

Now let us think it through. First of all, we learn from 1 John, "This is the assurance we have in approaching God: that if we ask anything according to his will, he hears us. And if we know that he hears us—whatever we ask—we know that we have what we asked of him."[2] "According to his will." What is His will? We know now: It is that we be filled with the Holy Spirit. Who is the Holy Spirit? He is God, and God is love. So the Holy Spirit is love, and to be filled with the Spirit is to be filled with love. When we are filled with love, we are in God's will. Thus the life of love is the rationale and function of the inner life of the believer.

Let me tell you a story. Dwight L. Moody, the American evangelist of the last century, finished speaking at a service one evening when a man approached him. "Sir," he said, "I enjoyed what you had to say, but I don't feel the need for your kind of religion. I am working out my own salvation."

Mr. Moody replied, "Sir, you can't work out what hasn't been worked in!"

If the inner life of the believer is to have any reality, the love of God has to be worked in. An outpouring must take place, a working of the Spirit. Whether this takes place at conversion or later is not the point. The sap has to get into the branches before the tree can bud and blossom and bring forth fruit; and the sap of the Holy Spirit is love.

Let's assume, for the moment, that we are in that blessed condition of being filled with the Spirit. We have been filled with love. That is to say, there has been a supernatural impartation, a pouring out of divine love into our hearts, a tapping of the mighty force that controls and operates the universe.

What do we do with it?

We put it to work.

Most of us have someone in our family about whom we have said, "I'd give anything to see him come to Christ." Let's see what the New Testament says about that. In the seventeenth chapter of Mark's gospel we read, "Stuff your pocket full of tracts and go after him . . . Wither him with argument . . . Haul him to church . . . Quote Scripture to him by the yard . . . Send him a subscription to a Christian magazine . . . Hire a Gospel Blimp and spray leaflets on his rooftree . . . "

Of course it doesn't say anything of the kind because

there isn't any seventeenth chapter of Mark. But what does the New Testament really say about attracting people to Christ? Here's what it says: "Be filled with the Spirit."[3] And unless I am mistaken, that is another way of saying, "Try loving him — or her."

Let's check the record further. In Matthew 5 we read, "Love your enemies." That could include the people we know who are completely off in their theology.

In John 13 we read, "A new commandment I give you, that you love one another." And because it was a new commandment, Jesus promised to send the Holy Spirit who would enable us to do just that.

Again in John we read, "By this shall all men know that you are my disciples, if you have love one for another."

The love of the Spirit is not something we can pour into ourselves.

How is it that we don't often see this love mixed in with the protocol at our stated church gatherings?

In Romans Paul tells us, "Owe no man anything but to love one another." And he suggests to the Corinthians in a famous chapter that none of the gifts of the Holy Spirit, not faith, not miracles, not tongues, not commitment, not even martyrdom means a snap of the fingers to God without love.[4]

In 1 Timothy we learn that the end of Jesus' commandment is love, with no faking of it. In Hebrews we read, "Let brotherly love continue." First Peter says we are to have an unhypocritical love for each other as fellow Christians. No putting on; it must be real.[5]

James says that faith without works is dead. What is He talking about? What kind of "works"? Why, works of love, to be sure. What else? So what James is saying is that

97

faith without love is dead, which is exactly what Paul wrote to the Galatians: "Faith works by love."[6]

The purest epistle of love is 1 John. For example: "We know that we have passed from death to life because we love the brothers [and sisters]." And another: "He that doesn't love, doesn't know God." In his *Institutes of the Christian Religion* John Calvin wrote 458 pages about the knowledge of God, but he failed to quote this passage from the apostle John. Again, John tells us that we can never, never, never know God if we don't love each other! In fact, if we claim to love God without loving each other, we are liars, because it's stupid (that's my word, not John's) to think we can love someone we can't see, when we can't even love someone we do see.[7]

Finally, in 2 John we are told that the original teaching of Jesus was that we love one another.[8]

I am not about to discourse on all the various Greek words for love, with their different shades of meaning, because the subject isn't all that complicated. A child understands love. A pet understands love. There is a black long-haired dachshund of my acquaintance that looks like a burnt hot dog, but he knows what love is.

Do you have your theological ducks in a row? How is your faith? Are you on praying ground? Do you feel you and God are compatible? Great.

How is your hope? Do you look for the Lord's appearing? Are you ready? Splendid.

What about your love? How is that doing?

When I went to Winnipeg in December, 1971, I had a problem. I didn't think anyone knew about it. As a member of an evangelistic team, I tried to hide behind the Billy Graham mystique. Then some Canadian friends got hold of me and I faced up to my problem, which was a lack of love. I asked God to crucify me and to fill me with His Holy

Spirit.

What about you? Could you use a little more love?

There is no secret formula. I have shown you Scripture, and could have quoted a lot more. People tell me, "It's all very well for you to talk about loving people. You just haven't been treated the way I have."

Perhaps not, I tell them, but I did have a problem.

"Yes, but you haven't been insulted, you haven't been cheated, you haven't been humiliated, you haven't been neglected, you haven't been betrayed."

And I tell them, maybe I haven't, but Jesus was. He went through it all, and He still loved. So did Paul and Stephen and many another New Testament Christians. And in the files of mission societies today are stories of Christians in Uganda, and Mozambique, and China, and Vietnam, and Nicaragua, and the Soviet Union, and the United States of America, who have been through it all, and because they have been filled with the Spirit, they still love.

Evelyn Thiessen, who with her husband Harry ministered to me during the Canadian revival, said, "God sent a divine solvent into my heart and dissolved all the bitterness I had built up toward my husband over twenty years." That same miracle can take place in any believing heart that is willing to put the love of God to work in relating to other people.

Human action won't bring it off. The love of the Spirit is not something we can pour into ourselves. And yet when we reach the point where we are willing to ask for it, He comes. How do I know? Because in God's Word it is stated that if we ask according to God's will, He grants our request. *Is love according to His will?* It is. We were made for the heights! But first, the cross. And that is why so much of the New Testament was written.

One other thought: How do I know? I speak after

the passing of years, because of something that happened to me.

PRAYER

Rock of Ages, Creator of our environment and lover of humankind, pour a solvent into my heart that will dissolve everything except the love You made into the poles and axles of the universe. Let me sit at the feet of my Master, Jesus Christ, and learn to apply His secret of love. And when I grow weary and wonder where it will all end, remind me that You are the End! In Your holy Name, Amen.

E·L·E·V·E·N

*How does the inner life of the believer
survive when tough times come?*

BATTLE
FLAGS

*When the enemy shall come in like a flood,
the Spirit of the Lord shall lift up
a standard against him.*
—Isaiah 59:19

As we make our way through this best of all possible worlds, strange things happen to us. We trip over our briefcase. A skylab slips its orbit and splashes into our swimming pool. The steering wheel of our car comes off in our hands. Ants appear in our cereal.

But it doesn't stop there. Before our eyes the earth may open and swallow us up. Insurance people like to tell us that disaster, calamity, and catastrophe can strike without warning and catch us off guard. We wake up one morning to find that the future, once so bright with promise, has disappeared forever.

How does the inner life of the believer survive when tough times come? The cause could be anything: a drunken driver on the freeway; a paralyzing fall off a ladder; a divorce; Alzheimer's disease; a maimed child; a stock market failure that involved lifetime savings; drug addiction or AIDS in the family; dismissal from work; false accusations; loss of reputation and standing; a robbery; a physical beating; an airplane crash; fire, flood, typhoon — the list could go on and on.

Does it make sense to talk of tranquility and serenity under such conditions? We are not thinking now about distractions or minor events that make interesting conversational pieces; rather we are asking what happens to the private castle of our soul when real tragedy breaks over us. Can we (to paraphrase Kipling) keep our head when all those around us are losing theirs and blaming it on us? It seems almost a mockery to assume that when everything falls apart, one can still retire to a secret place of composure and peace of mind. What we need is damage control.

This chapter is not a "how-to" manual on "coping cheerfully with chaos." Rather, it aims to put the arm on the inner life; to see whether what we have been talking about will stand up under pressure when one's personal situation seems to collapse.

Visitors from abroad who have toured the great castles and cathedrals of Europe may have noticed the battle flags that decorate the halls and naves of the historic buildings. The precious emblems are not too exciting to outsiders, but to the combat veterans who took part in the engagements where those flags were carried into the fighting zone, they have become colorful symbols of living history. What memories they evoke! What trials! What dangers! And — what victories!

I have strolled through the castles of Chillon, and Dover, and the Tower of London, and wondered at the displays of flags. I have observed the faded and occasionally tattered banners hanging in Edinburgh's St. Giles

Cathedral, and thought of the battles of Marston Moor and Culloden, and the "Scots, wha hae wi' Wallace bled." But now I am thinking of a different kind of battle—yours and mine. And I am asking whether in that private castle of ours there is not a room, perhaps the chapel, where we can hang our own battle flags. Could not those devastating events that so radically changed the direction of our lives be turned into trophies? They would remind us that even though we have been through the heat of bloody combat, and have the scars to show for it, we are still here by the grace of God, and can prove it. Behold our flags of battle!

The apostle Paul was not ashamed to point to the trophies he had acquired in his efforts to take the gospel to an indifferent and hostile world. He wrote of stonings, and lashings, and shipwrecks, and betrayals, and hardships that make most of ours seem puny by comparison.[1] Yet in his inner life he was able to live in a contented frame of mind.[2] He seems to have had a trysting place with his Lord, a citadel in his heart that renewed and refreshed him. How else could he have maintained his poise aboard ship when captain, crew and passengers were panicking in the storm, as related by Luke in the Book of Acts? How else could he have survived hunger, cold, nakedness, hostility and treachery, and lived to write 1 Corinthians 13? God gave his servant a private castle, and filled it with battle flags. What names they bore! *Philippi . . . Iconium . . . Lystra . . . Jerusalem . . . Rome.*

The Letter to the Hebrews tells of other believers who were driven to the end of their resources, yet found something extra—something the New Testament calls "faith"—that nourished their inner life and gave them victory through Christ. As the roll is called for these magnificent heroes of the past, and we learn how they were mocked, stoned, flogged, tortured, chained, sawed in two, and all the rest, we can almost see the battle flags waving, and hear the shouts of Hallelujah.

That brings it back to you and me. When the big blow strikes, how does it leave us? It could be anything—physical, psychological, spiritual, emotional—that happens to us. Whatever it is, it shatters us. We look about desperately for an escape shaft, some way out, but there is none. In our funk we pick up a Bible and whip through it looking for favorite passages. We read that there is an "amiable tabernacle," a "balm in Gilead," a secret closet where we can be alone with God, and the trials of this life will not loom so large. We try to find this place. We set aside time for prayer, and ask God to tell us what to do. But our prayers are feeble, and our hearts are red and torn, and even the verses we love seem to us remote.

And how does God respond? He points us to the cross. He tells us there is no way back, or over, or under, or around, but there is a way through. But we're not satisfied. We feel there has got to be an escape chute to somewhere, so we can get away from it all. We must find relief where the world cannot intrude. The drunk has his bottle; what do we have? Maybe there is a castle where we can hoist up the drawbridge, drop the portcullis, slam the gate and find refuge from the awful thing that has happened to us.

Is there such a place? Yes, there is a castle, a stronghold, a fastness, and the Lord is there; but spatial it is not. To learn what it is really like, we have to look at a different kind of enemy who is capable of assault more deadly than anything yet mentioned.

In our age of high technology it is not considered rational or relevant to speak of the demonic; yet no other word adequately describes the force that introduced to our own century the cruelties that sent millions of human beings to their death by the gas chamber or slow starvation. At the same time no other word properly explains the corrupted soul of an individual who has elevated self to the place of God. Supernatural wickedness can and does invade human personality; that is a fact of life.

The proliferation of demon worship throughout the world in the 1970s and 1980s is also a known reality; but my aim is not to measure the activity of Satan. Rather it is to make clear that evil forces can and do attack the inner life of the believer, and (more important) to show how these forces can be neutralized and rendered impotent.

When Jesus was attacked by Satan in the wilderness, according to the Gospel account, our Lord was fasting at the time.[3] I have found that God will honor a fast at a time of extraordinary stress. Yet fasting is a human activity, and when one is assailed by the principalities of darkness, and is spiritually wounded and bleeding, no human effort is strong enough to drive back the enemy.

If the Bible teaches us anything, it teaches us that death is not the end of the story.

Only one weapon will contain the onslaught and hurl the demonic forces back into the pit. That weapon is the Word of God. Jesus' only defense against the devil was to quote Scripture. When we realize how weak and ineffective we are, how powerless to cope with the kingdom of evil, we can fall back on the divine revelation in Scripture and find relief. The name of Jesus still sends the hordes scattering in disarray. I have been attacked by the devil in the pulpit, and have tried in vain to shake the evil thoughts from my mind. Then I remembered the words of our Lord, "Without me you can do nothing."[4] When I finally realized that I was powerless to fight back, and that my defense was totally out of my hands, the comical side of the situation became apparent, and I began to relax. My spirit revived, and the attack ceased and has not returned. Something like that may have happened to Martin Luther in the Wartburg Castle when, according to tradition, he threw an inkwell at the devil. The inkstains are still there; another battle flag!

It is right for the believer to hate the devil, because the devil is hate. But when other people act "devilishly" toward us, our response is to be the opposite. We cash the check of Romans 5:5; the love of God is poured out into our hearts by the Holy Spirit which is given to us. In other words we are to love them, forgive them, and then drop the subject. When we do that, our castle gate is wide open, and we can go in and out at our pleasure, for the Lord is there. We can even go into the chapel, and find there that a new battle flag has been hung.

Satan has one more arrow in his quiver, which the apostle Paul named "the last enemy."[5] For millions of people, including many Christians, death has become the greatest catastrophe and the ultimate tragedy of life. Many a believer's inner life has dried up with the approach of death. The castle of the soul becomes a ruin, uninhabited, deserted. Yet if the Bible teaches us anything, it teaches us that death is not the end of the story.

At Calvary our Lord Jesus Christ won a supernatural victory over the last enemy. He made sport of the principalities and powers of evil. On the third day He rose from the grave and is alive today, and that is not all, for we believe that in Him and through Him and by Him we too have eternal life.

The late John S. Whale wrote, "Belief in the Resurrection is not an appendage to the Christian faith; it is the Christian faith. The Gospels cannot explain the Resurrection; it is the Resurrection which explains the Gospels."[6] That being the case, our Christian view of death can never be the world's view. In the garden of Joseph of Arimathea the last enemy was conquered. When our loved ones die, we mourn our loss at the time; we weep over our separation from them; we honor their memory. But as believers in Christ we know what lies ahead, and it is all joy and celebration. Even the death of a young person means only the temporary interruption of love.

During World War II Ernest Gordon, a captain in the 93rd Scottish Highlanders, was captured by the Japanese at sea and taken to a prison camp on the river Kwai in Thailand. After three and one-half years as a prisoner, he was released. The book he wrote, *Through the Valley of the Kwai,* left a permanent mark on me. In it he told the story of an Australian prisoner, a private soldier, who was caught by Japanese guards outside the fence of his prison while trying to obtain medicine from the Thais for his sick friends. He was summarily tried and sentenced to death. I quote the rest of the story from Dr. Gordon's book:

On the morning set for his execution he marched cheerfully along between his guards to the parade ground. The Japanese were out in full force to observe the scene. The Aussie was permitted to have his commanding officer and a chaplain in attendance as witnesses. The party came to a halt. The C. O. and the chaplain were waved to one side. The Aussie was left standing alone.

Calmly he surveyed his executioners. Then he drew a small copy of the New Testament from a pocket of his ragged shorts. He read a passage unhurriedly to himself. His lips moved but no sound came from them. What that passage was, no one will ever know. He finished reading, returned the New Testament to his pocket, looked up, and saw the agitated face of his chaplain. He smiled, waved to him, and called out,

"Cheer up, Padre. It isn't as bad as all that. I'll be all right."

Chapter Eleven

He nodded to his executioner as a sign that he was ready. Then he knelt down, and bent his head forward to expose his neck.

The Samurai sword flashed in the sunlight.[7]

I like to think that somewhere in the halls of heaven, battle flags are hanging in honor of Jesus Christ Himself; and that whenever "the saints come marching in" before the throne of God, they walk underneath those blood-stained banners. I also like to think that in some odd corner of the heavenly palaces a flag hangs, honoring an obscure Australian private soldier who taught us what it means to possess forever the inner life of the believer.

PRAYER

O Savior to whom I owe the gift of life, gird me against big trouble. Daily I am informed of others' catastrophes. After I have sincerely prayed for the sufferers, I can't help wondering what I would do if their troubles were mine. God, I am not up to it. Help me! Give me the Excalibur of the Spirit that will overcome every conceivable calamitous circumstance in your victorious Name. Amen.

T·W·E·L·V·E

No greater need exists among Christians today than to have a fresh filling of God's love in their inner lives.

SOUL FOOD

It's about time we cut out the theological grand opera and got back to practicing the scales.
—*Vance Havner*

For the moment let us pass up discussion of castles and battlements while I pose a direct question: Are you ready to lay hold of God? To get a grip on Him? Because if you are, something has to be done to fortify the inner life. Not so long ago believers used to speak familiarly about the "soul." Many do not realize that the word *psychology* itself comes from two Greek words meaning "the study of the soul." Today the word *soul* is missing from the index of textbooks on psychology, and even many Christians wonder if there is such a thing. That's why we will stay with the term, *inner life*. So, how to fortify it?

To sustain physical life, dieticians tell us, three basic types of food are required: proteins, carbohydrates and fats. Without such nourishment the body will wither and become an anemic, shrunken thing. If the believer's inner life is to be healthy, it requires the same kind of daily upkeep as the physical life. The intake of food, the disposal of waste, rest, exercise, mental activity, social relationships—everything the body needs every day, could be said of the inner life as well.

The New Testament gives us three qualities that make up the nutrients of the healthy inner life. They are faith, hope and love. These elements traditionally have been called virtues, but they are more than that. They are the meat of spiritual existence. We shall place them under the glass briefly.

Faith

Instead of making a theological statement about faith, let me pass along a story that Sam P. Jones, the Southern Methodist evangelist of the last century, used to tell. (To understand it, you may need to be reminded that a hundred years ago to "get religion" meant, in parts of America, to give one's heart to Jesus Christ.) Here is Sam Jones speaking:

A man who lived down in middle Georgia a number of years ago, a very intelligent man, young and married, went to church one day. His wife didn't go with him. When he came home his wife said, "What sort of meeting had you today?"

"A pretty good meeting. I joined the church today."

"Have you got religion?"

"No."

"What did you do that for, if you haven't got religion?"

"The preacher said if I would do before I got religion as I would do after I got religion, I would get religion."

"Well," said she, "if that doesn't head me. You

joined the church, and haven't got religion!"

That night just before they retired, he said, "Wife, get down that old Bible; I am going to pray at home."

"Are you going to pray when you haven't got religion?"

"Yes."

In the morning he said, "Get that Bible, wife; I am going to pray again."

"What do you pray for without religion?"

Wednesday night he went to prayer meeting in the country, and they called on him to pray. He got down and did his best; and his wife said, when he told her he had prayed at the meeting, "You pray in public, sir, and got no religion! What did you do that for?" But he moved along on that line about three weeks, and the first thing you know religion broke out on him all over, from head to foot.[1]

This amusing story illustrates perfectly the two sides of faith: man's side and God's side. From the human standpoint, Mr. Jones's gentleman was obviously sticking out his neck by pretending to be what he was not. We have all heard people in public life use religious terminology, and have wondered whether they were putting us on. But Mr. Jones's man was evidently sincere; he was what they used to call a "seeker," and he was exercising a faith he wasn't quite sure existed. He was going out on a limb.

God, on the other hand, was ready to take the man at his word, and to honor his prayer even though it left something to be desired. The Letter to the Hebrews says that "faith is being sure of what we hope for and certain of what we do not see." But this man wasn't sure at all; and yet God rewarded him with faith. Our tentativeness may look and sound pretty flimsy, but it looks great to God, because He is the Rock.

I love Sam Jones's story because something quite similar happened to me. I grew up without any real interest in or knowledge of the gospel. After marrying into an evangelical family I suddenly began using words like "grace" and "redemption" and "blood" without really knowing what they meant or what I was talking about. I did it because I knew there was a thinness to my liberalized brand of Christianity and wanted desperately to deepen my faith; but the way of salvation was still a foggy mystery to me. People explained it to me, but I just couldn't buy it; even so I kept on using the words. I still don't understand what happened, but there came a time when I awoke to an awareness that the fog had dissipated; that certainty had somehow replaced uncertainty; that the words I had been using were light and truth to my inner being, and that I was a child of God's kingdom, saved by faith.

Once the gift of faith has been bestowed, it seems to lift the believer above the paradoxes, incongruities, and baffling contradictions of life. The good hand of God is seen in everything, no matter how wretched the situation may appear on the surface. This is what so exasperates the unbeliever. He cannot see why the Christian cannot face up to reality as he sees it. When a dam burst in Georgia a few years ago, causing death and destruction at Toccoa Bible College, a reporter asked the college president how he squared the tragedy with his belief in a loving God. He replied, "Who am I? What right have I to challenge the action of my sovereign Lord?"

There is a cosmic "Nevertheless!" to faith. It challenges the otherwise inexplicable with a "Yes, but . . . " It believes in spite of the evidence to the contrary, because it believes God is greater than the evidence. Day by day, hour by hour, faith supports the inner life of the believer. We go by simple truths: "God said it, Christ did it, I believe it, that settles it." It is not only that we are saved by faith; this same faith carries us and sustains us all the way through our planetary pilgrimage.

Faith is sometimes called an extension of reason into the unknown. It is spoken of as a risk, but to the Christian that is a misunderstanding of trust. Faith is grounded not on wishing, hypothesizing, gambling, surmising, guessing, speculating, or whistling in the dark, but rather on the Word of God. Faith believes that God means what He says in the Bible; as my friend and mentor, Robert Munger, told his students, "The New Testament will do what it says it will do." On that rock of certitude the believer can rest; on that diet of solid food the inner life will receive nourishment. The believer can lay hold of God, and God will not let down His friend.

Hope

Of all the responses of which the human spirit is capable, hope is one of the finest. It is hard to imagine the inner life of anyone, let alone a believer, without hope. In the New Testament hope is often, but not always, related either to the resurrection of Christ (our "living hope") or to the second advent of Christ (that "blessed hope"). We find such an emphasis in Romans 5:2: "We rejoice in the hope of the glory of God."

I would like however to examine with you the sentence that immediately follows that verse. Let us take it first in the familiar King James version: "And not only so, but we glory in tribulations also, knowing that tribulation worketh patience; and patience, experience, and experience, hope; and hope maketh not ashamed . . . "

Now let us look at these words in the light of the original Greek. The Greek word translated "tribulations" (or in the NIV, "sufferings") meant originally a compressed or narrow way, so that a modern rendering could very well be "pressure." No one living in the twentieth century needs to be told what pressure is. This condition, says the apostle Paul, leads to what the King James version calls "patience" and the NIV "perseverance." But the original Greek word was a combination of two words, which when translated separately mean "remain" and "under." When the pressure is on, the Christian is enabled to "stay under" the situation. That ability suggests "staying power." In more modern terms, when the heat is on, we "hang in there." This in turn creates what the King James version calls "experience" and the NIV "character." Again, the Greek word Paul used actually means a "testing" or "trial" or "proving." Thus pressure induces staying power, and staying power is road-tested for performance.

Finally, the proving out of one's staying power under pressure creates the conditions for hope—and it is the kind of hope (as the NIV correctly translates) that does not disappoint. That is to say, it is no barren hope; it does not leave us shamefaced.

What Paul is saying to us is that the hope that sustains the inner life of the believer is not some wishful expectancy that "everything will turn out all right." It would be nice if it did, but Murphy's Law still operates on this less-than-perfect planetary orb. Valid Christian hope has to go through the whole cycle; it is given a complete checkout, but it comes through performing brilliantly because it is built on faith in a living God.

Christian hope has a smile on its face. Why not? For the believer, life is full of anticipation and the future looks great. Every morning brings a fresh blessing from God. Don't let the expert theologians tell you that the only hope expressed in the New Testament is for the return of Christ and the rapture of the church. That is indeed our hope, but it is not our only hope. Take another look at the famous eleventh chapter of the Letter to the Hebrews. It relates dramatically what the great leaders in Israel's history did "by faith," but let me assure you that if there had been no hope among those leaders, there would have been no faith. Hope is what leads to faith and trust.

In our private castle, about which we have been thinking, one of the most important rooms is the armory. Here the weapons of our warfare are forged and polished. The apostle Paul writes to the Ephesian Christians in a famous passage that they are to "put on the full armor of God" so that they can "take your stand against the devil's schemes."[2] But why would they do that, if they did not hope to be able to withstand the power of darkness?

---

*Hope is the greatest
of all motivators.*

Had Moses not hoped that God would part the waters of the Red Sea, as He said He would, Moses would never have stretched out his hand in obedience to the divine command. Had David not hoped that his stone would hit Goliath, he never would have put it in his sling. Had Bartimaeus not hoped that Jesus would heal his blindness, he would never have called out His name as he sat by the roadside begging. Had Paul not hoped that he and the others on shipboard would be saved, when everyone else had lost hope, he never would have cheered the crew of the ship from Alexandria as he did. Hope is the greatest of all motivators. In the heart of a believer it quickly flows into faith, trust and confidence, but hope is what starts it all.

A football player faces a knee operation that could close out his athletic career. A doctor, through no fault of his own, finds himself caught up in a malpractice suit. A photographer is urged to save his business by making some quick money in "boudoir photography." A housewife comes home from shopping and, for the first time, is beaten by her husband. Each one is looking for a way out. Each one is grasping for hope. You, too, have a difficult situation to face, and you are looking for a sign of hope. What does the Bible have to offer?

Let the Lord of the castle lead you into the armory. Here you will find the belt of truth: Buckle it on. Next, put on the breastplate of righteousness; and for footgear, the gospel of peace. Now pick up the shield of faith, cover your head with the helmet of salvation, and grasp the sword of the Spirit. And then tell me, as you spur your steed through the castle gate, you who are facing a crisis—how is your hope?

Love

Television, which is making the greatest single impact on our culture, is doing its best to convince the human race that love will not work. Instead, it offers revenge, greed, pride, and lust as the correct motivators of human behavior. It is at this point that the Christian must stand "contra mundum"—against the world. We declare that love, as Jesus Christ, God's Son, revealed it, does work. The issue is joined, and no compromise is possible. We are to be filled with the Holy Spirit whom Jesus sent, for the Holy Spirit is love.

With this love, both faith and hope flourish, no matter how tragic the circumstances. Love penetrates every aspect of the inner life and fortifies it. Love is the beauty parlor both of the body and the mind. It brings out the best in us, and drives out the worst. It imparts meaning to everything, and without it there is no meaning. As for the gifts and fruits of the Spirit, they draw whatever quality they possess from love.

The devil may seem in control of much activity in this world, including the media; but God controls the universe, and God is love. The galaxies moving in their gigantic orbits are obeying the command of love. The sun sends its rays to planet Earth because of love. The supreme purpose of creation is love. Love is what sent Jesus Christ into the world. He lived for love, He taught love, He died for love; but His love proved stronger than death. The gospel He gave us is a love letter from God, teaching us to be rooted and grounded in love, as Paul says, so we can know the love of Christ and be filled with all the fullness of God.

No greater need exists among Christians today than to have a fresh filling of this love in their inner lives. We need to remember that the castle we have been looking at is a castle of love. It is not some ugly fortress with blood-stained walls and dungeons strewn with skeletons. It is a haven of warmth, with a fire blazing in the huge hearth, and songs and laughter and good cheer.

Love is tougher than elephant hide and harder than carborundum, yet at the same time it is an extremely delicate flower. It can withstand the gates of hell, but it can also be damaged by a cross look, an unkind word, a display of pride or a desire to hurt. Such damage is not beyond recall; it can be repaired and made new by the grace of forgiveness; and it has great tenacity. When human love is suffused with God's love in Jesus Christ, poured out into our hearts by the Holy Spirit, it can surmount anything.

Such love spills over into many aspects of life, and everywhere it brings blessing. It becomes charity, and people begin feeding the hungry and healing the wounds of society. It becomes romance, and hearts begin to glow with tender affection for each other. (I speak as a recent bridegroom.) It becomes adoration, and takes the form of music that lifts the hearts of millions of people.

Thousands of erudite books have been written about Christian love, and yet loving seems to come so hard for us. What keeps us believers from loving? Vance Havner said it's about time we cut out the theological grand opera and got back to practicing the scales. I find that prejudice, built in perhaps from childhood, keeps a lot of us from loving others. Or it may be pain; when people are in miserable health, they find it hard to be outgoing in love. Or it could be bitterness; we feel cheated, and ill-used, and frustrated, and we decide life is not worth the powder to blow it up. Love is a waste. How tragic that young people so quickly slip into such a mood, and end by destroying the gift of life God gave them.

On the other hand, I am convinced that the spread of Christianity throughout the world has been fostered more by love than by doctrine. People become Baptists and Pentecostals and Lutherans and members of different churches not simply because of preachers or choirs or traditional forms of worship or creed, but because they found love inside those walls.

What a wonderful thing it would be if a fresh outpouring of love struck our churches! What it would do for the inner life of us believers if once again our houses of worship were filled with the love that Jesus Christ exemplified and shared with us while on earth. Minstrels, where are you? Strike up the music. Flood the castle once more with the sounds of joy while we celebrate. Let the world see demonstrated in us the love it can never give—or take away.

PRAYER

O Giver of the granite of faith, the promise of hope and the sweetness of love, kindle a fire in me for the spreading of Your Word. Let the pages of Your sacred truth capture my soul. Show me that it is not my words but Your priceless, magnificent gospel that people want to hear, and absorb, and live by, through Jesus Christ our Lord.

T·H·I·R·T·E·E·N

*Our American Christianity tends toward
spiritual barrenness. We concentrate
on grandiose efforts to serve God, not
realizing that meanwhile our inner life
is in danger of shriveling.*

IN
v.
OUT

*The end of man is an action, and not a thought,
though it were the noblest.*
—*Carlyle*

Christ with me,
Christ before me, Christ behind me,
Christ beneath me, Christ above me,
Christ on my right, Christ on my left,
Christ where I lie, Christ where I sit,
Christ in every eye that sees me,
Christ in every ear that hears me.
—Old Irish Prayer[1]

A fellow Christian spoke to me recently about a mutual friend. "The amazing thing about Dick," he said, "is that he seems to see God in everyone he meets. He gives his whole attention to each person, whether it be a little child, an older person, or anyone." I happen to know Dick, and I agreed thoroughly with my friend's estimate of him.

But does seeing God in everyone, as our friend Dick seems to do, presuppose that everyone is godly or has god-like qualities? Of course not. Dick is a Christian. What he sees is a potential, something that was put in every human being by the Creator. Some may wish to define this potential: Is it "addressability" or "visualization" or the common grace of God? I don't know. But I do know that Dick's interest in and concern for other people is what the New Testament is all about. Jesus Christ is well named "the Man for others."

Seeing God in other people glorifies God Himself, and gives meaning, purpose and significance to the believer's inner life with God. Not that the inner life needs to be extraverted to justify itself! Being with the Lord is its own justification. But until the knight receives a commission in his castle and sallies out on his own knight-errantry, he is out of work. He is still a knight, but a knight with a rusty lance.

The tension between the inner life of the believer and his outer life has existed since the days of Mary and Martha. Always the temptation is to emphasize the one at the expense of the other. Let two stories help out here. The Reverend Forbes Robinson, an Anglican clergyman, died in 1904 at age thirty-seven, leaving behind a fragrant memory of holiness. After his death a friend wrote, "Forbes told me, 'As I grow older . . . when I desire to see the truth come home to any man, I say to myself, If I have him here, he will spend half an hour with me. Instead, I will spend that half hour in prayer for him.'"[2]

I personally would prefer to spend my half hour praying with the man in person, but I cannot compare myself to Forbes Robinson, who was a beautiful spirit. He felt that God could help his friend more than he himself could; and who are we to argue the point? I recall the words of a wise Scottish woman who told me, "A saint is a person who knows how to get out of God's way." It seems that Forbes Robinson's inner life had such a radiant quality that his letters were collected and published after his death, and are still being read.

On the other hand, Basil, the beloved bishop of Caesarea, who died in A.D. 379, was consulted on one occasion by the monk Hilarion. The monk informed his bishop that he intended to become a desert hermit and devote himself to prayer; whereupon Basil (who had himself once tried the solitary life) asked him, "Tell me, when you are out there by yourself, whose feet will you wash?"[3]

Here we have the twin dangers. Our American Christianity tends toward spiritual barrenness. We concentrate on grandiose efforts to serve God, not realizing that meanwhile our inner life is in danger of shriveling. We can't wait to get through "devotions" so we can get back to "accomplishing something" for Jesus. We even resent the time taken for prayer. We save our real energy for the nuts and bolts — large gatherings, significant events, projects, flowcharts, blueprints, surveys, financing, and blacktopping the church parking lot. Such is the case with too many of us. We have been sold on the idea that what is important is not time with God, but time working for God. The basic bond of fellowship between the creature and the Creator, which is the primal relationship of life, becomes an untied shoelace. Instead of securing the believer's footing, it trips him up.

The opposite danger is equally real. In this technological age some are going to extremes in their eagerness to provide "spiritual growth" for our inner lives. All kinds of complicated structural procedures are being devised to start us praying, fasting, sitting, standing, singing, vocalizing, meditating, worshiping, breathing, kneeling, and engaging in other sanctified activities (not to say acrobatics) that leave us dangerously close to exhaustion.

I freely admit my inadequacy in failing to meet such standards. I love to sing, to kneel, to pray, to worship, and even to breathe. In the middle of the night I love to meditate on the attributes of God: His holiness, justice, righteousness, goodness, wisdom, beauty, compassion, truth and love. Before I fall asleep I sometimes get as far as His omnipotence, omniscience, self-existence, perfection and everlastingness.

But my inner life rebels against all forms of regimentation. The directions seem so neat and helpful on

---

If there is to be spiritual growth...
it will come through our loving each other.

---

paper, but to put them into practice assumes an orderly house, and whoever said a Christian home was orderly? Halford Luccock used to speak of the home as a "divine disorder," which is about the size of it. When the telephone rings, or the dog bites a neighbor child, or the sink is plugged, or the car won't start, our schedule is out the window.

Jesus told us, "The wind blows wherever it pleases. You hear its sound, but you cannot tell where it comes from or where it is going. So it is with everyone born of the Spirit."[4] That is the real secret of the healthy inner life: It is free. It is not controlled by the Holy Spirit so much as it is set free by the Holy Spirit. It is like Lazarus coming out of the tomb. No doubt others were standing around (coroners, medical examiners, tax collectors, obituary editors, funeral directors) who would have much preferred that Lazarus stay in his grave and keep things orderly. But

Jesus said, "Loose him and let him go."[5] Take off the grave clothes and turn him loose! In the daring words attributed to Augustine, "Love God and do as you please."

The relationship of the believer's inner life to his outer life is further clarified by the words of the risen Christ to Peter in Galilee after they had finished breakfast by the lakeside. Three times our Lord asked Peter if he loved Him. It was a valid question, for only a few days earlier Peter had denied Him three times. Now, when Peter declared his unswerving love for his Master, the response came twice, "Feed my sheep," and once, "Shepherd my sheep."[6]

The message is clear: If the love we have toward our Lord is genuine, if the inner life is glowing, it will show itself not so much in spiritual exercises or manifestations as in the way we take care of each other. Growth is, after all, God's business. Jesus asked, "Which of you by taking thought can add a single cubit to his height?"[7] If there is to be spiritual growth, it will be the work of the Holy Spirit, and will not be conscious, any more than is physical growth. It will come through our loving each other.

A friend in Louisiana, Gwen Sanders, wrote these lines:

> Help me remember
> when others I see
> that they're reading the gospel
> according to me.

The gospel of Jesus Christ is an outgoing message by its very nature, and the purveyor of the message is the believer. It follows therefore that the believer's inner life is the messenger's reserve tank that provides the fuel for evangelism. The fuel itself is love, not zeal, or duty, or constraint, or a desire for stars in one's crown, but undiluted, unadulterated love—the love of God poured out in our hearts by the Holy Spirit to give us love for each other.

Chapter Thirteen

Anything less is a disguised ego trip and will prove self-defeating, for people quickly appraise and judge our human motives. They can understand that we think God's love is so wonderful that we cannot keep it to ourselves. What they cannot accept is insensitive human aggressiveness, disguised as "holy boldness," and condescending pride, which assumes we are better than they. Only when the inner life has spent time in the castle of the Lord does it learn to let the Holy Spirit's witness prepare the way before the human witnessing begins. And the witness of the Spirit is a witness of love.

It's as if our lives were a glass, and the Lord had a golden pitcher filled with living water, drawn from the artesian wells of infinity. He wants to fill that glass so it will spill over and fill other glasses. Unfortunately He can't fill our glass. Do you know why? Because there is already water in it, and it is dirty water, full of sediment. That glass has to be turned upside down and emptied out before the living water can fill it. That emptying is what the New Testament calls being crucified with Christ. The pouring of the living water from the pitcher is the filling of the Holy Spirit. It is He, and not the devoutness of our human striving; it is He who sets the heart beating in the inner life of the believer.

Regardless of the lack of perfection among its messengers, of course, the work of spreading the gospel of Jesus Christ has to go on. Even if we knew for sure that the curtain of history would ring down tomorrow, the love of God would compel us to spend today evangelizing. The inner life has to get out!

The whole vast missionary enterprise of the Christian church, which has built such a marvelous global fellowship in the gospel, is nothing but the outward expression of the inward faith and love of God's sons and daughters. Let us call off some of the names: Columba, Kentigern, Patrick, Ansgar, Ninian, Ulfilas, Xavier, Eliot,

Nommensen, Schwartz, Carey, Judson, Morrison, Williams, Livingstone, Underwood, Coillard, Goforth, Strachan; and Mary Slessor, Amy Carmichael, Gladys Aylward, Mildred Cable, Isabel Kuhn, Ruth Paxson and Corrie ten Boom.

What a marching line of saints! And these were just a few of the tens of thousands who went all over the world publishing the glad tidings of salvation in Jesus. In the nineteenth century the average life span of a missionary arriving on the west coast of Africa was four months. And still they came, and still are coming. What inner lives they must have enjoyed, and still enjoy, with Jesus, the Master of the Keep and the Lord of their castles!

C. S. Lewis once implied that the most important thing in the world is the salvation of a human soul.[8] Substitute the word "least" for "most" and his statement will capture the world's total approval. Evangelism has an extremely low priority in society as a whole; the number of jokes about soul-winning evangelistic preachers must run into the hundreds. Yet the fact remains that each new generation must be won to Christ, or Christianity will become extinct; God has no grandchildren. The winning is the work of the Holy Spirit, but the task of announcing the good news of new life, and persuading the people to hear and respond, is ours. It is a clumsy business, for we Christians are not of the same high quality as our Leader or His product; but we have been commissioned to the task, and jokes or no jokes, we must be about the Master's business. "The church exists by evangelism as fire exists by burning."[9] Without it, the church is nothing but a private club, and not the best club in town either.

This is not a book about coming to Christ. It is about the quality of our life with Christ after we have come to Him. My arrival in the kingdom of God was most undignified; I was dragged in while a student in a liberal

125

theological seminary by evangelical members of my family, (to paraphrase C. S. Lewis) kicking and screaming and with eyes darting in every direction. It took some time for the Holy Spirit to penetrate the miasma, but that He did is the most important fact of my life.

What brought me to Christ was not forced periods of prayer, or sessions of Bible study, or spiritual handbooks, or powerful sermons in churches (though they certainly didn't hurt). What brought me to Him was the inner life of certain believers that I saw expressing itself in love toward me. I know of nothing more important to the work of evangelism than the fostering and nurture of that inner life.

And now let us assume that for us the vigil in the castle is ending. The knight has received his accolade and his mission. It is time to raise the portcullis, lower the drawbridge and open the gate, for we shall be riding.

PRAYER

Tell me again, Gracious Sovereign of my heart, that it is the love I show, rather than the words I speak, that attracts people to You. O radiant Source of light and truth, let the "Gospel According to Me" be clear and shining, and let all the honor be Yours, through Christ my Lord.

*A touch of class! That is the way the
believer's inner life expresses itself.*

A
TOUCH OF
CLASS

*Jesus said, "Lo, I am with you always." That is
the word of a Gentleman.*
—David Livingstone

This book has asked a lot of questions. Exactly what is
the inner life of the believer? What is it for? Assuming
it has a functional purpose, what makes it work? Is there
some semantic doubletalk or theological hairsplitting that
makes it possible for the inner life to co-exist with the pressures of earning a living amid the noise, the heat, and the
corrosion of life in the 1980s and 1990s? In other words, is
peace with God really possible in a sinful world? For
answers we have looked to the Scriptures of the Old and
New Testaments. Now we are asking what may prove the
most important question of all: How is this inner life lived?

In childhood many, if not most, of us were touched
by the stories of "when knighthood was in flower." No

doubt the ideals of courtesy, gallantry and honor attached to those days have been exaggerated out of all proportion in the telling. Human nature does not change that much from generation to generation. Cervantes was right to mock the escapist chivalric folklore of his day with his hilarious tale of Don Quixote de la Mancha. But the concept of moral strength in shining armor does not die easily; and the qualities of manhood and womanhood that come through in the traditional tales of knight-errantry carry an appeal that is perennial. As George Gordon Coulton has observed, "Many of the noblest precepts of the knightly code were a legacy from former ages, and have survived the decay of knighthood as they will survive all transitory human institutions, forming part of the eternal heritage of the race."[1]

Many times in the writing of these pages I have asked the question, "How does the believer live out his life with God?" Each time my imagination takes me back in time to the days of chivalry. I am kneeling in the chapel of a great castle, and the atmosphere around me is imbued with the spirit and flavor of knighthood. I see the battle flags above me and hear the distant music of the minstrels. And each time I seem to receive the answer to my question from the Lord of the castle Himself: "How is the believer to live out his inner life? *With a touch of class.*"

I open my Old Testament and find examples of the same courtesy, gallantry and honor that marked the age of chivalry. King David showed much kindness to the lame son of his friend Jonathan and the grandson of his late enemy Saul. He invited the young man to eat at the king's table for the rest of his days, and restored to him his grandfather's property.[2] Boaz, the Israelite farmer, showed generosity toward the newly-arrived young Moabite woman, Ruth, in an age when Moab and Israel were mortal enemies. He protected Ruth from the field hands and gave her the choicest field of grain to glean.[3]

The New Testament is replete with illustrations of the touch of class in human behavior. Jesus' stories about the Good Samaritan and the Prodigal Son are especially rich. The Samaritan takes the victim of robbers to an inn after binding up his wounds, and arranges to pay all charges, present and future. The prodigal's father, an icon of the heavenly Father, does not lay down the law to his son when he returns, but throws a party in his honor.[4]

John the Baptist told people, "If you have two coats and you meet someone who has none, give him one."[5] Jesus said give him both coats.[6] Jesus also said if a soldier forces you to carry his gear a mile as Roman law stipulates, instead carry it two miles.[7] When a woman interrupted a dinner party by breaking a jar of expensive ointment over Jesus, and Judas complained of the expense, Jesus said, "Let her alone. She has done a beautiful thing."[8] When He knew He was to be betrayed, His response was to wash His disciples' feet, including the feet of the one who would betray Him.[9] On the cross His final thoughts were not just for Himself but for others.[10]

A touch of class! That is the way the believer's inner life expresses itself. Gallantry — magnanimity — chivalry — polish. As we read through the New Testament we encounter it again and again. The apostle Paul showed the most delicate tact in dealing with the problems of the Corinthian church. Not heavy expressions of piety; not stern rebukes; but gentle reason couched in genuine love. When he returned a runaway slave to his owner, Paul asked the owner to welcome the slave as a brother, adding, "If he stole anything from you, I will make it up to you. Charge it to my account."[11]

But let us keep the record straight. Classic behavior is not limited to people with an inner life with God as we know it and as the New Testament describes it. Jesus often found goodness in strange places where the motivation of faith seemed to be lacking. In the history of the church the conduct of pagans has often put so-called Christians to shame. I always admired Socrates' behavior when he was sentenced to die by the Athenian court and ordered to drink a cup of poisonous hemlock. As his friends gathered to hear his final words, instead of inveighing against his accusers, or feeling sorry for himself, he turned with cup in hand to his friend Crito and said, "I owe a cock to Aesculapius. Take care of it."[12]

Since, however, we are interested in how the inner life of the believer is lived, let us look at some Christian examples. Alfred the Great, recognized as the noblest monarch in England's long list of kings and queens, was more than a benefactor to his people; he was a victorious warrior. For twenty-one years he led his troops in a bloody, drawn-out campaign against the invading Danes, until they finally gave up. He then summoned the Danish generals and invited them to remain in the land, with their families, and help him build the English nation. A class act! After recounting the other worthy deeds of this Christian king, the *Encyclopedia Britannica* concludes, "No monarch in history ever deserved more truly the epithet of Great."[13]

Francis of Assisi dismounted from his horse when he saw a ragged leper by the roadside, walked over, put his arms around him and kissed him.

During the days when "papists" were barely tolerated in colonial New England, John Eliot, the Puritan preacher known as the "apostle to the Indians," entertained a French Jesuit missionary in his Roxbury home for six weeks.

Henrietta Mears, a Baptist school teacher in Minneapolis, was called in 1928 to be director of Christian Education at Hollywood Presbyterian Church in California. She never married, and she became known as a person who did everything with class. She placed flowers in all the empty rooms of the huge church. She arranged parties for her college-age young people that reportedly surpassed the class parties at the University of Southern California and the University of California at Los Angeles. She traveled around the world inviting prominent Christians to come to her student conferences. Eventually she sent four hundred men and women into the ministry, one of whom, Dr. Robert Munger, ministered in Berkeley at the time I pastored a small church there. He was extremely kind to me. *What's different about this man? What makes him tick?* I would ask myself. One day I read Henrietta Mears's life story, and found out. Like his teacher, he had a touch of class.

Class is not a show; it may simply be a kind word or a sincere and genuine gesture.

When the world thinks of class it thinks of finery, polish, ostentation, elegance, lavish display, pomp and ceremony. It thinks of big cars, expensive perfumes, beautiful clothes and elaborate homes. Television has made it almost impossible to think otherwise. The appeal to sight and hearing is invariably to impress and dazzle. But it is all for the outer life, not for the inner. What matters to the inner life is not the appearance, the smell, the taste, the touch, or the sound. What matters is what lies behind it all, the motivating spirit in which a thing is said or done, the effort to go above and beyond the "call of duty" to help someone. Class is not a show; it may simply be a kind word or a sincere and genuine gesture. It is, as Jesus put it, the cup of cold water.

Well, what is keeping us from this kind of behavior pattern? Obviously it is admired, both by believers and unbelievers. As a lifestyle it is so impressive that people try to imitate it. Then why don't we try it? Give it a go!

The first objection is that we can't afford it. To do things up with polish, to make princely gifts, to put on a class act is frankly beyond our means. That however won't stand up against the gospel story of the widow and her two mites.[14] The have-not world is full of beautiful stories of class behavior in tight circumstances.

A second reason why Christians fail to rise to the level of chivalry is that so many are frustrated and disappointed with life. They live in the land of "if only." If only they had gone to a different school; if only they had not made such a dumb marriage; if only they had taken that other job when it was offered; if only they had driven a different route—the list is endless. The problem is that there is no land of "if only." It is a phantasm, a trap of Satan to destroy our inner life with God.

Still another obstacle is resentment. We are so full of bitter thoughts that the pure and beautiful thoughts can't get through. We find it hard to understand why someone else has it so easy, and our lot is so hard. I find the life of Abraham Lincoln to be an excellent primer for those who are frustrated and resentful, and cannot find their way to an inner life with God. This man knew virtually nothing but disappointments, yet he became the most beloved of all the American presidents.

But the best of all books to teach us how to find the inner life, and how to live it, is the Bible. It has been called a love letter from God, and to read the Gospels of Matthew, Mark, Luke and John is to sit at the feet of a Man who taught us all we need to know about the inner life. He said when He left the earth that He would send One who would stand alongside us and encourage us. His disciples taught us that this One is the Spirit of Love, who would dwell in us and be greater than any other force in the world. His apostle left us a manual of the inner life in 1 Corinthians

13, and Paul made it clear that the love of God is more than a gift, it is a "way," a "more excellent way" — the way of class.

Our study began with the picture of a castle, with walls, a moat, turrets, a great hall, an armory, and a chapel, and all the appurtenances of a mighty fortress. This, I suggested, is where the inner life of the believer is lived, with the Lord of the castle, who is the heavenly Father, and the Master of the Keep, who is our Lord Jesus Christ. No one can penetrate this castle except the believer himself; no evil thought or influence can break through the walls. Here the Christian can find his life orientation; here he can come to himself; here he (or she) can draw on revelation and inspiration to live in the outer world in a way pleasing to God.

But there is one other Person dwelling in the castle who must be mentioned, because He is the one who will go with the believer outside the gate and across the drawbridge into the world of men and women. That Person is the Holy Spirit. He is not some strange impersonal force; He is a Person to be trusted. When Christians say that Jesus is their friend; that He walks with them and talks with them; and that He lives within them; they are speaking of the ministry of the Holy Spirit.

It was to send the Spirit of Truth into the church that Jesus ascended to heaven. It was the Spirit's arrival that brought about the miracle of Pentecost; and it was His continued presence that enabled the church to survive through the centuries, to correct itself, and to spread the blessings of Christ throughout the world. Today everything true and beautiful and good that happens in the body of Christ which is the church, is the result of the Holy Spirit working in the lives of believing men and women.

But now I must leave you to your castle, for it is time for me to enter my own. As you cross over the drawbridge and enter through the portcullis and the double doors, it is my prayer that the Spirit of God Himself will meet you. As you explore with Him the mysteries of the inner life, may you be filled with love — love for everyone and everything except the power of evil. Then won't you come out and tell us about it? Let the whole world know what you have found — it may be what the world is looking for without knowing it. And may the blessing of God the Father, the Son and the Holy Spirit rest upon you.

PRAYER

Beloved Majesty, Ineffable Beauty, thank You for the moments You have condescended to spend with me in these pages. What a superb Communicator You are! To a world full of rancor and wickedness, You show a heart of love. To a suffering humanity quagmired in its self-made misery, You offer salvation in Your Son Jesus — with a touch of class. And now, Glorious One, would You please request the guard at the gate to lift the portcullis and lower the drawbridge? I am leaving the castle — but not You! Unless You go with me, it's no deal. But if there is anything You want me to do in that world out there, and You equip me and help me, I'll do it. They may laugh; they may misunderstand; I may fall on my face; it doesn't matter.

Now one more favor, Lord, if You please. Command that sentinel on the ramparts to sound a blast on his trumpet. See, I have grasped the two-edged sword of the Spirit which is the Word of God. Hallelujah! Clear the way, everybody, we're coming through.

NOTES

Chapter One: Your Private Castle

1. Job 13:15.
2. Cf. Lamentations 3:22-23.
3. The story is found in an old Latin biography of Tauler (1300-61), probably written by Rulwin Merswin, a Strasbourg merchant who gave away his wealth and became a spiritual protégé of Tauler. In 1857 it was translated by Susanna Winkworth and then republished in London in 1925 as "The History and Life of the Reverend Doctor John Tauler."
4. Cf. Matthew 13:44-46.

Chapter Two: The Love of the Spirit

1. R. Lejeune, *Christoph Blumhardt and His Message* (Rifton, N.Y.: The Plough Publishing House, 1963).
2. Ecclesiastes 1:2 (NIV).
3. J. D. Douglas, ed., *Let the Earth Hear His Voice* (Minneapolis: World Wide Publications, 1975), p. 281.
4. Cf. Erwin Lutzer, *Flames of Freedom* (Chicago: Moody Press, 1976).
5. Genesis 43:34.
6. 2 Corinthians 4:7.
7. Luke 23:42.

Chapter Three: The Fourth Tree

1. Shakespeare, "Hamlet," Act 1, Scene 5.
2. Luke 12:32.
3. Romans 12:3 (Phillips).
4. Romans 7:18 (NIV).
5. Shakespeare, "Macbeth," Act 5, Scene 3.
6. The full quotation from Lady Julian (1342-1413) reads: "Everything has its being by the love of God; that is, God made all things for love, and by the same love he keeps them." *Revelations of Divine Love*, Grace Warrack, ed. (London, Methuen & Co., 1958; first published 1670), pp. 10-11.

Chapter Four: Down v. Up

1. Patrick of Ireland.
2. Thomas à Kempis, *The Imitation of Christ* (London: Hodder & Stoughton, 1979), p. 25.

3. Francois de la Mothe Fénélon, in *Christian Perfection,* Charles F. Whisted, ed. (New York: Harper & Row, 1947), p. 205 f.
4. Samuel Taylor Coleridge, *The Devil's Thoughts.*
5. Bertrand Russell, *Power, a New Social Analysis* (New York: W. W. Norton, 1938), p. 11.
6. John R. W. Stott, *Christ the Controversialist* (Downers Grove, IL: Inter-Varsity Press, 1978).
7. Mark 10:43-44 (NIV).
8. 1 Peter 4:12.

Chapter Five: Up v. Down

1. Proverbs 16:18.
2. 2 Corinthians 11:30, 10:17 (NIV).
3. 1 Corinthians 15:9, 1 Timothy 1:15.
4. Reinhold Niebuhr, *The Nature and Destiny of Man* (New York: Scribners, vol. 1, 1941), pp. 190-91.
5. *Harper's* Magazine (November 1987), p. 49.
6. Romans 1:28 (NIV).
7. *A Theological Word Book,* Alan Richardson, ed. (London: SCM Press, 1950), p. 176.
8. Genesis 3:5 (NIV).
9. James 4:6, 1 Peter 5:5.

Chapter Six: The First Love

1. 1 John 4:11.
2. John 20:31.
3. Matthew 6:33 (NIV).
4. "Ichabod" is a Hebrew expression meaning "no glory." It is translated, "The glory has departed" in 1 Samuel 4:21.

Chapter Seven: The Great Distraction

1. Hebrews 2:18 (NIV).
2. J. Trevor Davies, *Sublimation* (London: Allen & Unwin, 1947), p. 116.
3. Romans 12:19.
4. C. G. Jung, *Psychological Types* (London: Routledge & Kegan Paul, 1949).
5. Westminster Shorter Catechism (1648), Q. 1.
6. Cf. J. Trevor Davies, *Sublimation* (London: Allen & Unwin, 1947).

Chapter Eight: The Other Kind of Prayer

1. Wirt & Beckstrom, *Topical Encyclopedia of Living Quotations*

(Minneapolis: Bethany House, 1982).

2. *Confessions of Augustine in Modern English,* tr. S. E. Wirt (Grand Rapids, MI: Zondervan, 1986), p. 10.

3. Dewey's definition of education as "the continuous, purposeful reconstruction of experience" was an attempt to denigrate the value of transmissive (i.e. traditional) educational systems. It became the philosophical basis of the writings of George A. Coe and other pre-World War II American religious educators.

4. Isaiah 59:16.

5. 1 Timothy 2:1.

6. Norman P. Grubb, *Rees Howells, Intercessor* (London: Lutterworth Press, 1952).

7. From the *Journal of George Fox*, ed. by Percy L. Parker (London: Isbister & Co., 1903).

8. William Law, *A Serious Call to a Devout and Holy Life* (Grand Rapids, MI: Eerdmans, 1975), pp. 255-271.

9. A. J. Gossip, *In the Secret Place of the Most High* (London: Independent Press, 1947), pp. 136-164.

10. Isaiah 1:15.

Chapter Nine: When God Says 'Wait'

1. John Milton (1608-1674), sonnet "On His Blindness."

2. Abbott-Smith, *Manual Greek Lexicon of the New Testament.*

3. Charles Spurgeon, *Lectures to My Students* (Grand Rapids, MI: Baker Book House, 1984), p. 174.

4. Charles Williams, *He Came Down from Heaven* (London: Heinemann, 1938), p. 25.

Chapter Ten: What Is the Inner Life For?

1. Stephen Vincent Benét, "John Brown's Body," in *Selected Works,* vol. 1, (New York: Farrar & Rinehart, 1942), p. 187.

2. 1 John 5:14-15 (NIV).

3. Ephesians 5:18.

4. Romans 13:8; 1 Corinthians 13:1-3.

5. 1 Timothy 1:5; Hebrews 13:1; 1 Peter 1:22.

6. James 2:20; Galatians 5:6.

7. 1 John 3:14, 4:8,20.

8. 2 John 5.

Chapter Eleven: Battle Flags

1. Cf. 2 Corinthians 11:23-27.

2. Cf. Philippians 4:11.

3. Matthew 4:2-3.

4. John 15:5.
5. 1 Corinthians 15:26.
6. John S. Whale, *Christian Doctrine* (New York: Macmillan, 1942), p. 73.
7. Ernest Gordon, *Through the Valley of the Kwai* (New York: Harper, 1962), pp. 105-06.

Chapter Twelve: Soul Food

1. Samuel Porter Jones, *Sermons and Sayings,* ed. by W. J. Leftwich (Nashville: Southern Methodist Publishing House, 1885).
2. Ephesians 6:11 (NIV).

Chapter Thirteen: In v. Out

1. Incorrectly attributed to Patrick. This prayer's origin is lost.
2. Forbes Robinson, *Letters to his Friends* (London: Spottiswoode, Ballantyne Co., 1920), p. 29.
3. Cf. *The Life and Times of St. Basil the Great as revealed in his Works* (Patristic Studies No. 57, Washington, D.C., 1939).
4. John 3:8 (NIV).
5. John 11:44.
6. John 21:15-17 (NIV).
7. Matthew 6:27.
8. Lewis's actual words were, "The Christian knows from the outset that the salvation of a single soul is more important than the production and preservation of all the epics and tragedies in the world." (*Christian Reflections,* Grand Rapids: Eerdmans, 1967, p.10.)
9. Attributed to Emil Brunner, the Swiss theologian.

Chapter Fourteen: A Touch of Class

1. *Encyclopedia Britannica,* 1953 ed., art. "Knighthood and Chivalry," vol. 13, p. 433.
2. 1 Samuel 9:1-13.
3. Ruth 2:1-17.
4. Luke 10:29-37, 15:11-32.
5. Luke 3:11.
6. Luke 6:29.
7. Matthew 5:41.
8. Cf. Matthew 26:10.
9. John 13:5.
10. Luke 23:34, John 19:26-27.
11. Author's translation of Philemon 18-19.
12. Plato, *Phaedo,* 188a.
13. *Encyclopedia Britannica,* 1953 ed., vol. 1, p. 591.
14. Mark 12:42.

Index

A

Aesculapius, 130
Alfred the Great, 130
Anger, 62-63
Ansgar, 124
Arthur, King, 29
Augustine of Hippo, 73, 123, 137
Aylward, Gladys, 125

B

Bartimaeus, 115
Basil, Bishop of Caesarea, 121, 138
Beatles, 40
Benét, Stephen Vincent, 95, 137
Bible, 30, 51, 69, 72, 74, 89, 93, 99, 104, 116
Blumhardt, Christoph, 19, 135
Boaz, 128
Brunner, Emil, 138

C

Cable, Mildred, 125
Calvin, John, 98
Canadian Revival, 22-26, 135
Carey, William, 125
Carlyle, Thomas, 119
Carmichael, Amy, 125
Cervantes, Miguel de, 128
Chalmers, Thomas, 72
Coillard, François, 125
Coleridge, Samuel T., 39, 136
Columba, 124

Coulton, George Gordon, 128
Cromwell, Oliver, 41
Cross, 23, 26, 30-31, 39, 99, 104
Crucifixion, 23, 31-33, 42, 47, 98, 124

D

David, King, 115, 128
Davies, Trevor, 62, 136
Dewey, John, 74, 137
Donne, John, 61
Douglas, J. D., 21, 135

E

Edstrom, George, 39
Eisenhower, President Dwight, 95
Eliot, John, 124
Eliot, T. S., 69
Evans, Louis, Sr., 72

F

Faith, 98, 110-13
Fear, 63
Fénélon, François de la Mothe, 38, 136
Forsyth, P. T., 72
Fox, George, 77, 137
Francis of Assisi, 130

G

Gesswein, Armin, 79
Goforth, Jonathan, 125
Goliath, 115

Good Samaritan, 129
Gordon, Ernest, 107, 138
Gossip, Arthur John, 77, 137
Graham, Billy, 42, 78-80, 98
Greed, 63-64
Gregory of Nazianzus, 54
Grubb, Norman P., 75, 137

H

Hallesby, Ole, 72
Hardy, Thomas, 33
Havner, Vance, 109, 117
Hilarion, 121
Hill, Rowland, 72
Hitler, Adolf, 48
Humility, 37-43
Holy Spirit, *passim*
Hope, 98, 113-16
Howells, Rees, 75, 81, 137

I

Ichabod, 59-60, 136
Intercession, 74-81
Isaiah, 74, 101

J

Jeremiah, 46
Jesus Christ, *passim*
Job, 13, 42
John, Apostle, 54-55, 57
John the Baptist, 129
Jonathan, 128
Jones, E. Stanley, 62
Jones, Samuel Porter, 72, 110-12, 138
Judas, 129

Judson, Adoniram, 125
Julian of Norwich, Lady, 34
Jung, Carl Gustav, 65, 136

K

Kennedy, President John, 94
Kentigern, 124
Kipling, Rudyard, 102
Kuhn, Isabel, 125

L

Law, William, 53, 77, 137
Lawrence, Brother (Nicolas Herman), 72
Lazarus, 122
Lewis, C. S., 125, 138
Lewis, Sinclair, 65
Lincoln, President Abraham, 95, 132
Livingstone, David, 127
Love, 22-23, 76, 98-99, 116-18, 132
Luccock, Halford, 122
Lust, 64-65
Luther, Martin, 11, 13, 106

M

Marriage, 67
Mears, Henrietta, 130
Milton, John, 84, 137
Mohammed Ali, 40
Montgomery, James, 71
Moody, Dwight L., 96
Morrison, Robert, 125
Moses, 115
Munchhausen, Baron von, 76
Munger, Robert Boyd, 113, 131

Index

N

Niebuhr, Reinhold, 49, 136
Ninian, 124
Nommensen, Ludvig, 125

O

Origen, 54

P

Palmer, Glenda, 70
Patrick of Ireland, 37-38, 135, 138
Paul, Apostle, 33, 46, 49-50, 64, 68, 95, 97, 103, 106, 129
Paxson, Ruth, 125
Pentecost, 34, 87
Peter, Simon, 41, 123
Plato, 138
Pope, Alexander, 68
Prayer, 71-81
Pride, 47-52
Pride Council, 48-49
Prodigal Son, 129

Q

Quarles, Francis, 29
Quixote, Don, de la Mancha, 34, 128

R

Ravenhill, Leonard, 72
Resurrection, 106
Revival, 22-23
Richardson, Alan, 51, 136
Robinson, Forbes, 120-21, 138
Russell, Bertrand, 40, 136
Ruth, 128-29

S

Sanders, Gwen, 123
Satan, 14, 105-06, 116, 132
Saul, King, 128
Shakespeare, William, 32
Shelley, Percy Bysshe, 49
Simeon, 86-87
Simeon Stylites, 81
Sin, sinner, 11, 30, 37-38
Slessor, Mary, 125
Smith, Fred, 40
Socrates, 130
Spenser, Edmund, 30, 45
Spurgeon, Charles H., 90, 137
Stalin, Josef, 48
Stott, John R. W., 41, 136
Strachan, R. Kenneth, 125
Sublimation, 67-68

T

Tauler, John, 15
ten Boom, Corrie, 19-21
Thiessen, Harry and Evelyn, 99
Thomas à Kempis, 38, 135

U

Ulfilas, 124
Underwood, Horace, 125

V

Van Dyke, Henry, 57
Vaughan, Henry, 72

W

Waiting, 83-91
Whale, John S., 106, 138

Index

Williams, Charles, 90, 137
Williams, George, 41
Williams, John, 125

X
Xavier, Francis, 124

Z
Zwingli, Ulrich, 77